BLACKMORE
PARK
In World War Two

BLACKMORE PARK

PARK

In World War Two

 AN ACCOUNT OF THE US ARMY HOSPITALS AT BLACKMORE PARK, MALVERN 1943–45

Fran and Martin Collins

BREWIN BOOKS

First published by
Brewin Books Ltd, 56 Alcester Road,
Studley, Warwickshire B80 7LG in 2008
www.brewinbooks.com

ISBN: 978-1-85858-428-7

A Cataloguing in Publication Record
for this title is available from the British Library.

Typeset in Sabon
Printed in Great Britain by
The Alden Press.

Contents

Introduction – Blackmore Park vi

Chapter 1 – 19th General Hospital: Humanitate Ministro –
   To Serve Humanity 1

Chapter 2 – 19th General Hospital – American Red Cross 16

Chapter 3 – Blackmore Park Site Two – 65th and 90th General Hospitals . .27

Chapter 4 – 12th Hospital Center 38

Chapter 5 – 93rd General Hospital 48

Chapter 6 – 93rd General Hospital – Special Service Section and
   Red Cross Unit 64

Chapter 7 – 155th General Hospital 71

Chapter 8 – 155th General Hospital – Convalescent Section 89

Chapter 9 – 155th General Hospital – Special Service Section and
   Red Cross Unit 97

Chapter 10 – Welcome in their Country 110

Chapter 11 – Ships that Pass in the Night 123

Chapter 12 – A Fond Farewell 129

Abbreviations 147

Glossary 148

Appendix 1 – American Military Units known to be in Malvern 1943-45 . .149

Appendix 2a – Army Hospital Centers 150

Appendix 2b – U.S. Army Hospitals in U.K. August 1944 151

Acknowledgements 152

Introduction – Blackmore Park

Blackmore Park in Malvern, Worcestershire, has seen a number of changes since its first recording in history in the thirteenth century. Together with Hanley Park, Cliffy Woods and four smaller woods; Baldenhall, Cleves, Bruerne and South Wood it comprised the Malvern Chase. The Chase belonged to the Lords of Hanley Castle, which was built around 1210 as a hunting lodge for King John.

In the middle of the fourteenth century Blackmore (or Erlesmore) park became a deer park, it was bought in 1548 by John Hornyold I who was a descendant of Edward III and who later also bought the manor and vicarage of Hanley Castle for £450. At the end of the fifteenth century the castle fell into disrepair. Most of the stonework was demolished and sold off, apart from one of the towers which survived until 1795. Nowadays the village of Hanley Castle stands on the site and the only parts of the castle which remain are the dry moat and a mound which stands near the church.

When the civil war broke out in the seventeenth century John Hornyold II stood for the king. He was killed at Worcester in 1643. His son, Thomas, had two thirds of his estate seized. After the Restoration he petitioned Charles II to reinstate his lands.

In the eighteenth century the Hornyolds, who were Catholics, built a large manor house at Blackmore Park called Blackmore Mansion which had numerous priest's hiding places. In the nineteenth century this was pulled down and rebuilt in a Jacobean style by John Vincent Gandolfi, a nephew of the Hornyolds, but un-fortunately this building was badly damaged by fire in 1880 when a servant set fire to a curtain with a candle. The house was rebuilt in 1881-83. In 1918 John Vincent Gandolfi died and his heirs divided up the estate and sold it in 500 lots across two days in May 1919. In 1920 the house burnt down again and all that remains is the front porch which is now part of Malvern St. James Girl's College.

Blackmore Mansion. (Malvern Library)

In World War One the estate had been used by the British forces and afterwards it was used intermittently for military purposes, serving in peacetime as a summer camp for the Territorial Army.

Part of Christopher Greenwood's 1822 map of Worcestershire. (Courtesy of Malvern Public Library)

During the early stages of the American involvement of the war in Europe, E.T.O. Chief Surgeon, General Paul R. Hawley, calculated that 90,000 hospital beds would be required to cater for American casualties from Operation Overlord and the ongoing campaign in Europe. Working towards this end the American forces requisitioned a small number of established British hospitals although most had already been set aside for the use of British troops. A number of owners of English country houses offered their homes to be used as hospitals for the American forces but few were suitable. It became necessary for the American government to plan a building programme for 116 hospitals, this figure to include 36 station hospitals and 16 general hospitals. Suitable hospital sites would need to be adjacent to water, gas and sewerage facilities with easy accessibility to roads and railways.

It was decided to build two 1,000 bed general hospitals on Blackmore Park. Work was begun on site on 6 October 1942 with a target date of March 31 1943. Various delays were encountered and the hospital was not completed until 30 July. The Demolition and Construction Company was the prime contractor and the Ministry of Works architects were on site to supervise the construction and to see that specifications of the contract were met. The British Royal Engineers took responsibility for the site from 19 August 1943.

Three other sites in the area were also set aside for U.S. hospitals, these being at Brickbarns, Merebrook and Wood Farm. Each hospital would specialise in

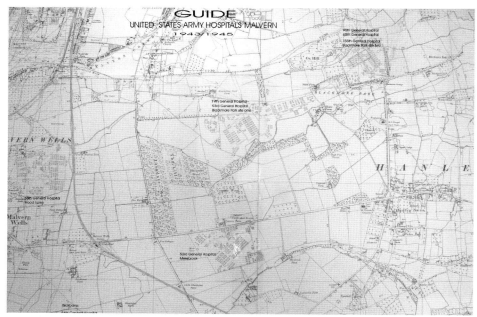

Reproduction of 1954 SO831424 and 1955 SO772417 Ordnance Survey map showing hospital sites. (With the kind permission of Ordnance Survey)

different types of surgery and treatment so that as patients arrived from the continent they could be sent to the hospital which would best deal with their needs.

The two hospitals at Blackmore Park were known as Plant 4172 (Site One) and Plant 4173 (Site Two). In September 1943 personnel of the 19th General Hospital moved onto Site One. In October 1943 the 65th General Hospital moved onto Site Two. In March 1944 the 65th moved to Botesdale in Suffolk and were replaced by the 90th General Hospital. In May the 19th moved to a holding station in Wales in preparation to set up a hospital in France and were followed in July by the 90th. The 93rd General Hospital took over from the 19th on Site One and remained there until the end of the war while the 155th General Hospital took over from the 90th on Site Two.

Although only a handful of hospital buildings remain at Blackmore Park, people in the local area still have strong memories of the American presence in Malvern and those who served or were treated at the hospital remember the area with fondness.

This book sets out the history of the two hospital sites at Blackmore Park, the part it played in the war effort and its impact on the surrounding area and its inhabitants.

Chapter 1

19th General Hospital: Humanitate Ministro – To Serve Humanity

In 1940 the United States Surgeon General requested that civilian hospitals play a part in organising military general hospitals for war duty overseas. This was because:

> *"It was believed that civilian medical personnel, having established a professional rapport among themselves in the course of their work would more quickly adapt as a group to war conditions."* (Rochester General Hospital Archives)

Rochester General Hospital, in New York, was one of the first hospitals asked to mobilise because of the exemplary service given by the hospital in World War One when it formed Base Hospital Nineteen.

Major General Magee, Surgeon General, assigned Colonel Wentworth, who was a veteran of World War One, as Commanding Officer of the unit upon mobilisation. Colonel Wentworth organised a professional staff of physicians, surgeons and dentists of whom 43 officers were affiliated with Rochester General Hospital. The staff was joined by a contingent of 80 area nurses under Chief Nurse Hazel Ventress. Of these 60 were alumnae of the Rochester General Hospital School of Nursing.

Thus the 19th General Hospital was activated in July 1942 in Rochester, New York, its motto being 'Humanitate Ministro' – To Serve Humanity. The advance party soon left for Camp Livingston, Louisiana, where it would be built up into a military hospital unit. Because the 19th had been formed from an existing hospital it

19th General Hospital

Emblem of the 19th General Hospital.
(Rochester General Hospital Archives)

was known as an 'affiliated' general hospital. This had certain advantages, as Dr. Fenstermacher of the 19th recalls:

> *"You never realised what a joy it was to be with all the people you knew and worked with from your home town."* (Rochester General Hospital Archives)

By August 1943 the unit was ready for overseas duty after undergoing training in combat intelligence, guarding military information, identification of enemy and friendly planes and treatment of tropical diseases. The detachment now consisted of 58 officers, 79 nurses and 500 enlisted men. An advance party went on ahead and the main group left on 29 August for destination 6616-SS-TAT – a military 'secret', although the girls working at the P.X. at Livingston informed members of the unit that the advance party had been seen in England.

On 5 September the unit embarked on a British ship, the HMS Scythia. Unfortunately on her last mission taking troops to North Africa she had taken two torpedoes in her bow and although she had been overhauled at Brooklyn Navy Yard she was unable to steam as fast as before. On this voyage she began to fall behind the rest of the convoy and it was necessary for her to return to port.

On 9 September she set sail again with a convoy of approximately sixty tankers and freighters moving at ten knots and following the usual zigzag course across the Atlantic. The convoy was flanked by destroyers and Canadian corvettes. Each day hydroplanes circled the convoy for a short time. Twice the convoy was attacked by submarines. One of the freighters caught a torpedo in her antisubmarine net and had to drop out of formation. The 19th didn't get to hear what happened to her but they did learn the next day that four freighters had been sunk in the convoy following theirs.

On board Colonel Wentworth was appointed senior medical officer and the 19th ran the Scythia's eighty bed hospital. While on board the personnel operated on an injured seaman, completed examinations, immunisations and treated venereal infections.

As the Scythia came in sight of the coast at Ireland she was released from the convoy and continued the journey alone until 22nd September when she anchored at Greenock in Scotland. Some of the men remember seeing two men submarines coming out of the port on their way to Norway. When they wrote to tell their relatives their letters were heavily censored. As the ship entered the dock the personnel were greeted by a Scottish band playing the bagpipes. At this point the unit was split into two, 35 officers and 310 enlisted men travelled to Malvern by train that day while the remainder were held on board ship until the following morning to cover any medical needs.

Meanwhile the advance detachment of two officers and three enlisted men had arrived in Malvern on 1st August. The date of 18th August was selected for

'Marching in' at Blackmore Park Site One. At the ceremony the British were represented by officials from the Ministry of Works and the Commander of the Royal Engineers. The U.S. Army was represented by the Base Section Surgeon, the District Surgeon and representatives of the Chief Surgeon of the European Theatre of Operations and the Commanding Officer of the S.E. district.

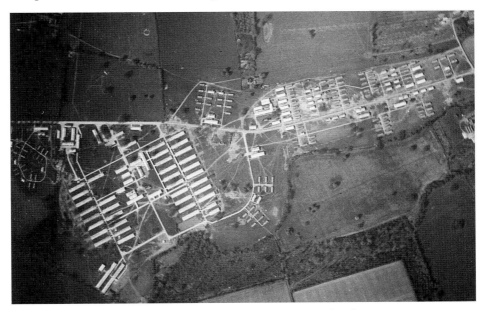

Aerial view of Blackmore Park Site One. (Rochester General Hospital Archives)

Unfortunately by August the hospital was not yet up to the standard required and it was decided that the U.S. Army would not accept the hospital as it stood:

> *"At that time the difference between the hospital as it stood and the plans as agreed on by both the British and American authorities was so great that it was decided that the U.S. Army would not accept the hospital as it stood."* (19th General Hospital Archives)

Reports from American engineers at the time indicated that the hospital was 98% complete, but there were many minor deficiencies and many missing items, principally equipment to be supplied by the British War Office. There was an absence of blackout curtains in certain buildings, faulty plumbing, poorly laid floor and incomplete installation of the water and sewage plant. The archivist for the 19th describes the site:

> *"The physical plant included 165 buildings in an area of sixty acres clinics, operating rooms and one story wards of tile and concrete and*

for barracks and quarters the half cylindrical wind tunnels know as Nissen huts. It was a British construction and inspection showed a number of things that failed to meet American standards, clinical arrangements, faulty plumbing, defective doors, lack of covered passageways and of screening in cookhouses and operating rooms. There were also shortages of equipment as a consequence of war's unlimited demands upon limited British resources." (19th General Hospital Archives)

It had been decided that all hospitals should have a dustproof floor so a pitchmastic floor was ordered for the buildings by the Office of the Chief Surgeon. Work was begun on the floors on 30 August and completed by the middle of November. The work on the floor caused complications as it was necessary to remove all doors, electrically heated food cabinets, tables, benches, racks and cabinets from the buildings concerned and then replace them when the floors had been completed.

The Lodge at the main entrance to Site One. (Rochester General Hospital Archives)

The Lodge 2006. (M.Collins)

Officers' Mess and ward buildings on Blackmore Park Site One. (Rochester General Hospital)

Administration buildings on Blackmore Park Site One. (Rochester General Hospital)

A detachment of men from the 52nd General Hospital at Wolverley had been sent to Blackmore Park to receive the stack of beds and mattresses for the wards. The remaining items to be furnished by the British were ordered immediately and the bulk of the order arrived during the fist two weeks of August. Unfortunately the supplies for the hospitals at Site One and Two came in one shipment and it was difficult to decide which items should be allocated to which hospital so everything was unloaded and stored on Site Two until it was decided how to divide it. Upon the

Surgical wards on Blackmore Park Site One.
(Rochester General Hospital)

arrival of the main group at the 19th in September the hospital was still incomplete. The archivist states:

> *"It was immediately obvious that a great deal of work was necessary to clean up contractor's litter from all over the area and to make some attempt to make the installation look presentable both inside and outside buildings. The pitchmastic floor layers were working and had another months work to do. There was a good deal of roofing, electrical wiring, carpentry and plumbing still in progress that delayed cleaning of buildings and disposition of supplies in buildings."* (19th General Hospital Archives)

As soon as each building was finished the personnel were assigned to it so that they could start work an adapting it to their needs and putting away supplies. The enlisted men built fences to keep trucks on the road and waste gravel was obtained to make road shoulders. Eventually, as the other hospital units arrived in the area, demand outstripped the need for gravel and cinders were used instead. Shrubs were obtained from local landowners to plant on the area around the headquarters and chapel buildings and fifty sheep were secured from a neighbouring farmer to remove the undergrowth of grass and weeds.

The arrangements for the electricity supply presented some problems as the standard current throughout the hospital was 230 volts whereas the hospital's American equipment was designed to operate at 110-115 volt. It was necessary to make adaptations so that the equipment could be used safely. The electrically heated food cabinets located in each ward kitchen also posed problems as when they were turned on the heat buckled the top and short circuited the heating element. Fortunately the maintenance electrician at the hospital was able to repair them.

George La Vine, a psychiatrist with the 19th oversaw the refurbishment at the site. He interviewed all the enlisted men to find out who had experience in carpentry. Major Fred Geib, the Special Service Officer sent trucks to one of the nearby supply depots, where equipment had been delivered in crates. The men were to collect the lumber from the crates to make shelves and furniture for the hospital. Office furniture, chairs, benches, tables, bedside stools, cabinets and shelves were constructed. Doors and windows were repaired and heating was installed in the latrine:

> *"A little matter not included in British blue prints."* (19th General Hospital Archives)

At this point the personnel believed that they would be stationed at Blackmore Park for the duration of the war so a number of officers went into Malvern to buy varnish and other items to finish off the furniture with their own money.

Apparently when an a officer from a nearby unit came to inspect the newly refurbished site he asked his Master Sergeant to make notes of everything the 19th had done so that exactly the same could be carried out in his hospital. At this time the men at the 19th had a saying:

> *"We may not be medics but we sure know how to be carpenters."* (19th General Hospital Archives)

The 701st Medical Sanitary Company, a black unit, consisting of 3 officers and 101 enlisted men was assigned to the hospital on 27th August 1943 to build the passageways and paved areas. From time to time detachments from this organisation were sent to other units to carry out labour. Those left at Blackmore Park were eventually divided among the two sites.

Because of segregation the black unit could not be quartered with the white personnel so on their arrival they were quartered on Site Two. With the arrival of the 65th General Hospital in October it was necessary for the men to evacuate this site and they were billeted in the three large V.D. wards and given the use of the patients' mess on Site One. One small building designated as an Isolation ward was turned over to them for Officers' quarters, headquarters, Post Exchange and supply storage. By December the patient load meant that the patients' mess was needed solely for the patients. Tented accommodation was considered for the black unit but it was thought that in winter this would be *'inhumane and unhealthful'* (19th General Hospital Archives). It was decided that the enlisted men would have

Inside the chapel of Blackmore Park Site One. (Rochester General Hospital)

to be attached to the detachment mess. Black personnel always had to stand at the end of the line so that there wouldn't be a mixture in seating. This also meant that 640 men were eating in a mess hall built to seat 198. The three black officers ate in the officers' mess.

Having black troops attached to the 19th General Hospital also caused problems in the town. Six of the men were attached to Detachment A, Company A of the 769th M.P. Battalion to be trained by and work with the M.P.s of that organisation in nearby towns in order to prevent trouble between black and white troops. Both chaplains at the 19th found it necessary to try and tactfully deal with 'racial problems' in their sermons.

The white personnel at the 19th were charged to:

> *"...in no way interfere with the British custom of allowing white girls to entertain coloured men."* (19th General Hospital Archives)

...which some, particularly those from the southern states, found hard to accept.

Shortly after the arrival at the 19th at Blackmore Park a detail was sent to Site Two to prepare for the arrival of the 65th General Hospital. A detachment of fifteen enlisted men was also sent on detached service at nearby Brickbarns to assist the 56th General Hospital to set up. Major Parnall also took a detachment of

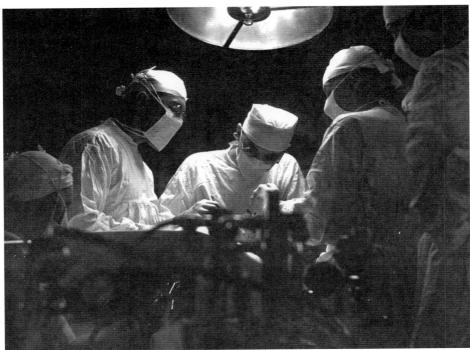

Dr.s Goldstein and Wood performing surgery at Blackmore Park Site One. (Rochester General Hospital)

officers, nurses and enlisted men to Rhyd Lafar, Glamorganshire to prepare a 750 bed station hospital for the 28th Infantry Division until its own medical facilities were established.

By 8 October it was possible to assign officers, nurses and enlisted men to three quarters of the wards and clinics and on 1st November 1943 the 19th General Hospital at Blackmore Park was finally opened to receive patients. The first out patients were received on 2nd November and the first ward patient was admitted on 3rd November. The first operation was performed on 11th November.

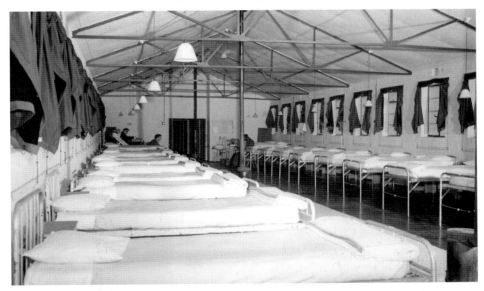

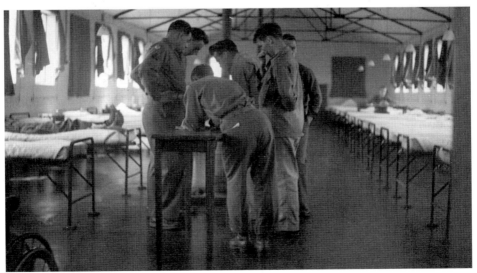

Patient Wards at Blackmore Park Site One. (Rochester General Hospital)

The majority of the patients were wounded airmen and battle casualties from Italy and North Africa. The hospital also catered for the ailments of the troops based in the U.K. including Northern Ireland. In December 1943 patients from the 79th General Hospital in Northern Ireland were air evacuated to Blackmore Park. Planes landed at nearby Pershore Airfield. In January 1944 Car Number 203, operated by Nurse Lieutenant Cook of the 45th Hospital Train Unit, was assigned to the 19th General Hospital for its use for transporting patients from the ports.

As the build up of American troops in the U.K. expanded more patients were admitted because of sickness or accidents. In February 1944 it was necessary to erect six ward tents and prepare the ground for 25 more to cater for the increase in patient numbers. Ambulatory patients requiring minimum care were placed in these tents.

Officers' Wards with ward tents at Blackmore Park Site One. (Rochester General Hospital)

The personnel of the unit found that they recognised some of the patients arriving at the hospital. Apparently when servicemen and women from the Rochester area of New York serving in the U.K. heard that the 19th was at Malvern they requested having their treatment there. Dr. Walter Fenstermacher remembers seeing a former female patient who had made her way to Malvern so that she could be treated by the same doctor who had treated her back home.

A large number of the personnel working at the 19th were volunteers from Rochester hospital, but a number of enlisted men had been drafted into the hospital to make up the numbers. Dr. David Parker remembers the court martial of one such man who had hit the officer in charge of the mess while arguing over cleaning the grease trap. He was court martialled and found guilty of striking the officer at a court martial in Cheltenham.

The Special Service Section of the 19th catered for the entertainment of the personnel while spending off duty time on site and various shows were organised for the men and women. The 19th had a projector and regularly showed movies. The Special Service also organised sports tournaments and constructed a softball diamond, volleyball and badminton courts and horse shoe pitching courts.

Off duty time was also spent in exploring the local area. The unit's first impressions were mixed. They found that:

> "...the tropical conditions under which we sweated it out in Louisiana were hardly ideal preparation for the fog and drizzle of the English Midlands. We were quartered in Nissen huts, tending stoves against the perpetual camp cold. In time we learnt to function around blackouts as well as drive 'on the wrong side of the road'." (19th General Hospital Archives)

Officers of the 19th Malvern. (Rochester General Hospital)

Officers' quarters at Blackmore Park Site One. (Rochester General Hospital)

Interior of Quarters at Blackmore Park Site One. (Rochester General Hospital)

On the other hand the archivist also reports that;

"It was fair indeed among the lanes and among the well kept farms of Worcestershire. The site of our hospital, Blackmore Park, had been the home for several hundred years of an old country family, the Hornyolds. The manor house had been torn down but the lime bordered approach remained, the nightingale sang in May and there were oaks that might have been contemporaries of the druids. The drones of Forts and

Lancasters carrying bombs to the Continent reminded us daily however of what country we were living in and why we were in England." (19th General Hospital Archives)

P38 flying over Officers' Mess on Blackmore Park Site One. (Rochester General Hospital)

On their arrival at Blackmore Park the 19th had been invited to a civic reception at the Winter Gardens in Malvern. Local dignitaries on hand to welcome the unit were the Chairman and Vice Chairman of the local council. A large number of prominent citizens like lady Beauchamp and Sir Ronald and Lady Lechmere were also invited to attend. The chairman, Mr. W.H. Grundy, made a speech welcoming the Americans who had:

> *"...come thousands of miles to help the old country in its effort to stamp out the evil which has arisen in Europe and also to restore the freedom of the enslaved nations."* (Malvern Gazette)

The Winter Garden's Orchestra played the Star Spangled Banner and God Save the King and then the evening took on a more informal atmosphere.

Later, Mr W. Powell, the headmaster of the Malvern Link Council School, felt moved to write to the 'Ohio Journal' in America to describe how he and his wife came to meet and get to know four American nurses at the Reception. Following this occasion Mr. Powell and his wife invited the girls to their home on several occasions including Christmas Day 1943. The couple became an honorary family for the girls while they were in the area.

Major Fred Geib, the Special Service Officer, arranged for the men to attend other functions put on by the local people. He managed to procure nearly a hundred second hand bikes so that the men could travel around the area. The doctors even used the bikes to make their rounds on the hospital site. Dr. David Parker remembers going on a cycle ride with colleague Frank Ford one day. He recalls them struggling to cycle up one of the steep Malvern hills when they were overtaken by an elderly lady on her bike. He remembers thinking:

"Boy what a great ad for the American officers." (Rochester General Hospital Archives)

Generally the personnel of the 19th were made to feel welcome by the people of Malvern. The archivist records:

"The small tradesman and Lord Beauchamp made us feel equally welcome in their equally unheated homes." (19th General Hospital Archives)

Surgical Wards at Blackmore Park Site One. (Rochester General Hospital)

When the men were invited out to dinner they would first visit the Mess Hall where they would be given food to share with the family that had invited them. Dr. Walter Fenstermacher remembers that Mr. Perrin, of Worcester Sauce fame, would often invite officers to his home. Walter remembers Mr. Perrin taking him and Lloyd Allen to visit the Royal China Works.

Some of the contacts with local people led to long-lasting friendships, some even to Anglo American marriages although a few led to indignant letters from girls' parents to Colonel Wentworth. The archivist notes that:

"The English girls, deprived of their own men, working long hours on farms and in factories, undated and often depressed by losses in battle and bombing were peculiarly vulnerable to the breezy American soldier with generous impulses and a pocket full of money." (19th General Hospital Archives)

In May 1944 the unit were given orders to leave Malvern and move to Colwyn Bay, a staging area in North Wales, where the 19th undertook lectures, demonstrations, close order drills and inspections. From here the unit moved to another staging area in Southampton and after three days crossed the channel in victory ships to land on Utah Beach on August 16th.

In France the hospital was attached to the American Third Army under General George S. Patton. The 19th set up a 1,000 bed hospital at Le Mans on 20 August in a French hospital recently vacated by German troops. For a month it was the furthest forward of any of the general hospitals, so close to the fighting that some of the wounded came directly form the battle lines.

In December part of the hospital followed the troops behind the front lines of combat and opened up a hospital in a French barracks at Nancy while some of the nurses were dispatched to Paris to cater for casualties from the Battle of the Bulge. In August 1945 the hospital moved to Marmelon and in September the unit sailed back to the U.S.

At the end of the war General Paul R.Hawley, the Chief Surgeon in the E.T.O. wrote to the parent hospital in Rochester to commend the work of the unit throughout the war. The 19th was commended for being:

"...a well trained unit, able to do the job without outside help."
(Rochester General Hospital Archives)

-32-

HEADQUARTERS
EUROPEAN THEATER OF OPERATIONS   prh/glc
OFFICE OF THE CHIEF SURGEON

ADDRESS REPLY TO: 1 July 1945
   CHIEF SURGEON E.T.O.U.S.A.
   A.P.O. 887

The Medical Director,
Rochester General Hospital
New York

Dear Doctor Parnall,

    One of my last and most pleasant duties as Chief Surgeon of the European Theater of Operations is to make of record the splendid service of the 19th General Hospital.

    This hospital unit first started to operate in this Theater 1 November 1943. It established first at Blackmoor Park, Worcestershire, England in one-storeyed Nissen huts which were later augmented by ward tents. The unit remained here unit moved to a staging area on 12 May 1944.

    For movement to the Continent after D-Day, I selected some of the best of the hospitals in the United Kingdom; and, of course, the 19th General Hospital was among the first to be sent to France. It landed on Utah Beach 16 August and set up a 1,000-bed general hospital at Le Mans on 20 August continuing there until 22 December of that year.

    As our Armies moved forward, it was necessary to follow them closely with general hospitals; and again the best we had were moved in close support of the fighting troops. The 19th General Hospital opened again, this time in a French barracks, in Nancy, on 15 February 1945 and it has remained there since.

    I find myself at a loss for words to describe the superb quality of medical personnel that came with this unit. I have had to draw upon this personnel to leaven weaker units in the Theater. Despite these drafts upon the personnel of the 19th General Hospital, those that still remain with the unit maintain the same high standard of professional care that characterized this unit on its arrival in this Theater.

    The 19th General Hospital provided an x-ray officer for the 1st Auxiliary Surgical Group, three surgeons for the 3rd Auxiliary Surgical Group and many specialists for other hospitals.

    The Rochester General Hospital can be very proud of the 19th General Hospital. It has rendered valuable service to our Country; and it has been both an official and a personal pleasure for me to have had this fine unit under my direction.

                    Sincerely,

                    P.R. HAWLEY
                    PAUL R. HAWLEY
                    Major General, USA
                    Chief Surgeon

Letter of commendation.
(Rochester General Hospital)

Chapter 2
19th General Hospital – American Red Cross

In November 1942, while the 19th General Hospital was training at Camp Livingston, Louisiana, it had put in a request for a Red Cross Unit. The unit of five girls was duly sent but unfortunately it was necessary to withdraw one of the girls, Mary J. Cunningham, the medical social worker and leader of the group. This incident generated much correspondence both within the Red Cross organisation and between the Red Cross and Colonel Wentworth, the Commanding Officer.

Mrs. Ione Hopkins, the Assistant Field Director of the Red Cross at Camp Livingston was sent to observe and interview the four remaining girls and Colonel Wentworth about the matter and then produce a report. Before the report could be published the Field Supervisor, Mrs. Marguerite Parsons, wrote to Miss Ruth Coon, Assistant Field Director of Military and Naval Welfare Service, American Red Cross, Eastern Area, advising her about the visit and explaining that Mrs. Hopkins had described the four remaining members as being incapable of their duties:

> "...because of the weaknesses of each member ... the success of the unit is doomed." (19th General Hospital Red Cross Archives)

She was also concerned that Colonel Wentworth was:-

> "...a very peculiar person, very difficult to approach and perhaps not entirely friendly towards the Red Cross." (19th General Hospital Red Cross Archives)

This information was completely contradicted by Mrs. Hopkins in her report as she wrote in it that she found the girls':

> "...personal and group strength so commendable." (19th General Hospital Red Cross Archives)

And Colonel Wentworth:

> "...*genuinely hurt and upset over the whole matter.*" (19th General Hospital Red Cross archives)

Although she does go on to say that:

> "*At no time during the five months of their stay here had he given his Red Cross unit a word of commendation, or exhibited any interest whatever in them.*" (19th General Hospital Red Cross Archives)

Colonel Wentworth justified himself by saying:

> "...*he was afraid of seeming to be interfering.*" (19th General Hospital Red Cross Archives)

Although Mrs Hopkins thought that this was:

> "...*farfetched.*" (19th General Hospital Red Cross Archives)

Colonel Wentworth put in a request for Mary Cunningham to be replaced in January and became impatient when she wasn't, especially when the Red Cross decided to withdraw the other four girls. He wrote to the Red Cross explaining how much he valued them, having served with them in France in World War One and that his wife did much Red Cross voluntary work. He finishes his letter:

> "*Furthermore this 19th General Hospital was originally organised in 1915-16 as a Red Cross hospital. I have been associated with it since its inception, so you had better be good to us.*" (19th General Hospital Red Cross Archives)

Two days later Colonel Wentworth received a letter saying that a Red Cross unit would be sent as soon as possible. The new one actually arrived in July just before the embarkation to England.

The Red Cross girls sailed with the 19th to England and then attended a course in London. They rejoined the 19th at Blackmore Park Site One on 29th September and were billeted in a Nissen hut along with the hospital dietician.

While awaiting the patients' arrival at the hospital the girls worked on making their quarters homely:

> "*This required shopping in the nearby towns and community for such a variety of commodities as tablecloths, dishes, Victrola records, radio,*

iron, yarn for making rugs and afghans, bicycles and a hundred and one other things. Thus equipped we spent hours making rugs, arranging and rearranging furniture to make our hut an inviting place. We believe our efforts have been rewarded and in spite of the limitations we now have a comfortable and cosy home." (19th General Hospital Red Cross Archives)

On October 29th the unit were able to invite the two Red Cross units from the neighbouring 65th and 56th General Hospitals for a 'house warming party'.

The Red Cross had also been assigned the half built isolation ward as an office, so in the early part of October the girls made plans for renovations to the building. When they approached Colonel Wentworth to discuss the renovations they found that the process was not going to be as easy as they first thought:

"We learned that in the army renovations aren't made so easily so sinks weren't removed, additional phones weren't installed and a tub remained in the secretary's office until a better use was made for it." (19th General Hospital Red Cross Archives)

On 25th October the floors in the building were finished and the girls could 'move in' although at the beginning packing cases were the only furniture they had. The Special Service supplied some furniture to the girls and also supplied lumber and manpower to build bookcases and other pieces of furniture on the understanding that Red Cross carpentry tools would be lent to the Special Service section to make the furniture they needed. Several months later the Red Cross were still attempting to reclaim their tools which had been used for various jobs across the hospital including making concrete walkways.

The Special Service also donated 4,000 books to the Red Cross which were to be catalogued and stored in the library. This was a massive task which the Red Cross completed by holding a 'library party'.

"Tables were set up in assembly line fashion for the party- glue pots, brushes and a supply of date due slips and card holder were on each table and an ample supply of books was placed within reach. Equipment was also set up for cutting more of the necessary slips. The boxes of unsorted books were opened and empty boxes were labelled." (19th General Hospital Red Cross Archives)

The Red Cross also set up a record library which was sorted and classified according to orchestra.

Once books were organised in the library a selection could be taken around the wards for the bed bound on a food cart but this was far from ideal. The Special

Service promised to make book carts but these were not completed until February. The Recreation report for February reads:

> "*We finally put our book carts into action and they have been enthusiastically received by the patients in the wards. They enjoy thumbing through the books and making their own selections. Their interest in reading was increased so much that we have requests for certain books which they'd like us to bring.*" (19th General Hospital Red Cross Archives)

Recreation Building. Blackmore Park Site One. (Rochester General Hospital Archives)

Officer's Club. Blackmore Park Site One. (Rochester General Hospital)

The Red Cross also had the use of the patients' recreation hall. Initially the hall was used mainly for movies and educational lectures but by the end of the year the Red Cross had acquired ping pong tables and a piano for the room. Unfortunately the concrete floor made the room cold and dusty. The hospital did assign a man to do the heavy cleaning in the Red Cross building and care for the fire. It also supplied the girls with a list of patients who would be able to do odd jobs for them.

At the beginning of November the girls were asked to assist the Officers Recreation Committee in decorating the Officers Club in readiness for its opening on November 7th. One of the girls made arrangements in Malvern to hire a piano and flowers were purchased in Hanley Swan and placed in tin cans which had been painted red, white and blue and decorated in silver with the insignia of the 19th General Hospital. The girls went out on the Malvern Hills to collect ferns and berries to decorate the walls and beams. The lights in the room used for dancing were softened by fastening pink crepe paper around the globes.

Prior to the patients' arrival in November the girls had discussed with Colonel Wentworth the scope of their recreation and social work programme. The Red Cross were willing to handle social case work but the Colonel made it clear that he did not want them getting into the realm of 'treatment' which he felt was the responsibility of the doctors and nurses. The Colonel outlined the programme he wished the girls to follow. One of the girls, Mary Maher reported that:

> *"he stressed the fact that we were working in an army hospital and that there was one authority or command and that he was it and that all work done in the hospital was done with his approval … He mentioned that a hospital run from and by a 'military point of view' is quite different from a civilian hospital. 'A man in the army is a fighting man and all efforts and concerns of the hospital personnel are directed towards making a man fit to fight', 'mercy' is out in a military hospital."*
> (19th General Hospital Red Cross Archives)

He felt that the Red Cross unit's role at the hospital was:

> *"…to help the soldier-patient by easing his mind about personal problems, writing letters for him and handling home problems and in no way to attempt the treatment of the patient."* (19th General Hospital Red Cross Archives)

He also told the unit that a craft programme would be unnecessary. The Colonel himself planned an army programme of shop work for the patients to do directed by his men as this was:

"...More manly and 'more army' " (19th General Hospital Red Cross Archives)

The Colonel was happy that the library had been set up because he felt strongly that men should further increase their intellect and their own resources through reading. He said that he deplored the fact that people were too dependent on being entertained and that more 'army teaching' should be undertaken in the wards. The Red Cross girls did try to point out that:

"...his was a high standard and many men did not have the inward resources to follow it but our program would and could be directed towards those ends but we would have to necessarily start at the patients standards." (19th General Hospital Red Cross Archives)

Planned recreation programmes by the Red Cross were to be presented to the Colonel in writing for his approval before they were posted on the bulletin boards. The girls had a programme of ward visiting which was approved although the Colonel stressed that the medical officer in charge of each ward should be consulted before visiting. The social workers and recreation workers planned to visit the wards daily, the social worker to visit and talk with each patient to find out their needs and the recreation workers to take books, games and records to the patients. At the request of the patients the girls put on victrola concerts of popular and classical musicals in three different wards.

The social worker was very much in demand on the wards to help the patients with various issues. A large number of men wanted to contact friends they had served with. Enquiries were even made about contacting people in occupied countries. Many patients needed help in contacting their units to reclaim their personal possessions and mail. In these cases the girls contacted the Red Cross Field Directors with the unit the man had been serving with.

The girls received enquires from the United States concerning the patients and personnel working at the hospital. Patients also asked the girls to contact the Red

Letter sent from a sergeant in the 19th General Hospital. (Author's collection)

Cross in their hometowns to find information about their families and children. One sad request was that a cable be sent to the United States on behalf of an officer who received news of the sudden death of his three year old daughter.

A happier result was achieved when a letter was received from a Red Cross Field Director asking the girls to inform one of the men that his brother was staying at a nearby Red Cross club. The man had not seen his brother for two years. The girls reported on the reunion:

> *"Several days ago Pvt. A strolled in the office with his double strolling after him. All we could see were two pairs of shining black eyes, two broad grins, two overseas caps perched on two dark heads. 'We're off until Sunday together, but we wanted to say thank you for all you've done'."* (19th General Hospital Archives)

The Red Cross also thought it important to make links in the local community around the hospital. They started by contacting and visiting Red Cross Clubs in the nearby communities and asked them to let the hospital know of any activities that could be attended by staff or patients. Letters were sent to twelve such clubs within overnight pass distance asking for their bulletins. Colonel Wentworth asked the girls to also gather information on nearby places of interest for tours for the enlisted men and patients.

The girls also made useful contacts with the ladies of the Women's Voluntary Service. Miss Day, the Executive officer, invited two of the girls to her home for tea and to discuss how the W.V.S. could support the Red Cross in their work at the hospital. The W.V.S. agreed to set up a hospitality programme, providing addresses of householders prepared to provide hospitality to the personnel of the 19th. The girls visited the homes to check their suitability and make dates. Unfortunately it was necessary to inform the W.V.S. that some of the homes were unsuitable. Initially this scheme did not work too well. It was not received enthusiastically by the men, who perhaps did not want to spend their one day off a week taking tea with a stranger. The girls reported:

> *"There is a reluctance on the part of the men to go and the Detachment Commander on his part, is seeing to it that only the gentlemen of the outfit represent us. ... Also because invitations were not accepted immediately did not mean lack of interest but that the men had only one day off a week and work other days until after 5, which rather interrupts the tea hour."* (19th General Hospital Red Cross Archives)

The W.V.S. were approached again in October when Captain Glenn from the 19th asked the girls to organise some entertainment for fifteen of his men who had been sent on detached service to assist in setting up the 56th General Hospital and for the advanced cadre of the 56th. At this point there were no recreational facilities on the post and the men were not allowed to leave the post. The W.V.S. was asked to select fifteen local girls to attend. The party on October 15 began with a movie and was followed by dancing and refreshments. Major Sharpe of the 56th laid on refreshments and transport to and from the post for the girls. (This was by ambulance – the only transport available.) At 11.30 the ambulances returned the girls to their homes and the first recreation service offered to the enlisted men by the Red Cross unit was thought to be a great success.

In November the girls were asked to help Special Service to plan a party for the enlisted men to be held in Malvern. The party was for personnel of the 19th, 56th and 65th General hospitals. The W.V.S. was again requested to distribute tickets amongst the local girls. Again the party was considered a success and it was decided that the three hospitals would take turns to give parties for the enlisted personnel in Malvern every two weeks.

Major Geib, the Special Service officer, decided to hold a weekly party on the post for the enlisted men in the Recreation hall. Colonel Wentworth requested that the Red Cross girls should act as chaperones, greeting the girls invited as guests, helping with the plans for the party and checking final arrangements. A detail of men cleaned the building, decorations were put up and the Red Cross provided music for dancing. It was reported that everything was ready but when Miss Johnson arrived, thirty minutes before the party started, she found that the victrola was unsatisfactory, the cloakroom was untidy and the refreshments had not been properly arranged for. The guests, thirty Wrens from Malvern, arrived at 7.30, but needless to say the party was not a great success. Afterwards the girls talked to the men about their lack of organisation and planning and it was decided that next time each platoon should take the responsibility for one aspect e.g. refreshments, entertainment, and that parties should be planned at least a fortnight in advance. The girls wanted to encourage the men to plan their own parties as they believed:

> "…the men must have a feeling that they are the hosts so that we may keep in the background and simply be on hand to offer any help that may be necessary." (19th General Hospital Red Cross Archives)

In the lead up to December the girls were busy planning Christmas events. Early in October the girls instigated the 'Post Exchange Christmas Shopping Service' and orders were taken from the personnel at the post. The girls spent one week in October sitting in the Mess Hall taking orders from the men. This gave the girls a good opportunity to meet and talk to the enlisted personnel as well as practice in handling British money on a large scale. About £300 was collected and although the gift list was limited the men appreciated the girl's advice on the appropriateness of gifts, especially for female friends and relatives. On October 11 two of the girls went to London to place their order.

Just before Christmas each ward was given a six foot Christmas tree and decorations including holly and mistletoe. A competition was held to find the two most attractive wards and the unit was swamped with requests for more paper, string, wire and lights. The judges: Chief of the Dental service, Chief of the laboratory Service and Chief and Assistant Chief Nurses made the rounds of the ward on the morning before Christmas to award the prizes.

The winning surgical ward used red and green powder paints to paint the lights above the beds. As the judges came into the ward the blackout curtains were quickly drawn and the men stepped to attention beside their beds. The tree was placed at the back of the ward decorated with streamers, bells, cut-outs from tin cans, cotton wool

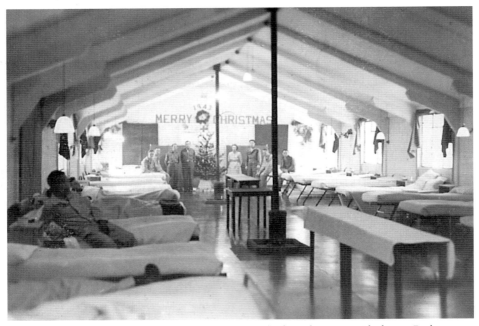

Christmas Decorations inside Ward 2 – the winning medical ward. Site One Blackmore Park. (Rochester General Hospital)

and a star at the top. The entire ward was festooned with streamers from the corners to the centre of the room and attached to each light shade.

The winning medical ward also used the coloured light bulbs effect. At the back of the ward the tree was placed in the middle of two red screens strung across the back of the ward was 'Merry Christmas' in two foot letters in red painted cardboard. Beneath the letters was a red cross of the same material. The bulletin board was attractively circled with holly and greens.

On the evening of December 23rd two groups of school boys came to sing carols on the wards. This was very popular with the patients and the boys were given many requests to sing. Several of the wards took up a collection of their candy and gum rations for the singers and one ward collected money to send the orphan boys a Christmas gift. On one of the wards one of the patients accompanied the two boys singing Silent Night with a guitar. The Red Cross noted that:

> "*Many of the patients remarked that the carolling was the nicest entertainment they had had in months and really made it seem like Christmas.*" (19th General Hospital Red Cross Archives)

On Christmas Eve 130 ambulatory patients attended a games party in the recreation hall. The hall was decorated with greenery and a large Christmas tree in one corner. As each man came into the hall he was given a sprig of green as a buttonier and was put into a team. The first game was 'pinning arms and legs on Santa Claus', the winning team putting together the best Santa Claus. The most active game of the evening was 'snowball fight' which involved opposing teams blowing ping pong balls off a ping pong table. Refreshments of sandwiches, hot chocolate and cake were served at the end of the evening and cakes and sandwiches were taken to patients unable to tend the party. After the party most of the patients left to attend carol services in the chapel.

Earlier gift boxes had been sent from London for the patients. The Red Cross girls decorated them with bright ribbons and sprigs of greenery and on Christmas eve they were delivered to the ward in a chow cart. They were left under the trees in the wards to be found by the patients first thing in the morning. The enlisted men of the unit also had a wrapped gift provided by the Red Cross and placed under the tree. For Christmas dinner table decorations were made in the shape of sledges with a packet of cigarettes hidden underneath. The patients unable to get to the mess hall had theirs delivered to their wards.

Shortly after Christmas a nativity play was presented for the patients in the recreation hall by a group of thirty children from the Elmville School Of Music in Cheltenham. About ninety men attended and afterwards the children were treated to hot chocolate, sandwiches and cookies in the Red Cross building while some of the patients helped serve and entertain them.

On New Years Eve the Red Cross held a bingo party. Because of its popularity this became a regular event every Saturday night. These parties were mainly attended by black personnel. The Red Cross girls noticed that if there were a large number of black personnel at events some of the white soldiers would look in but not stay.

In the following months the Red Cross organised several shows from outside groups and also attempted to put on patient shows. The first patient show was held in January but to their dismay the girls found that the performers who had spent time rehearsing the evening before were not the ones who actually performed on the night. In February there were two more patient presentation: 'Amateur Hour' and 'On with the Show'. There shows were better received due to more time and organisation being put in by the patients.

In February Colonel Wentworth allowed a limited craft programme to go ahead. He stated that:

> *"Distribution of craftwork supplied by the American Red Cross is limited to bed patients and ambulatory patients for use in 'off duty' hours."* (19th General Hospital Red Cross Archives)

One of the Red Cross offices was doubled up as a pressing room and craft room. The girls found that the leather work was the most popular craft followed by rug making. The girls noticed that often two or three men would work together on one frame. First they would make the looms, then the rugs, they rarely asked for instruction as they would teach each other. Square knotting and string craft was another popular craft with several belts being made. Some used string to make covers for their helmets and one patient used it to make a new pocket for the billiard table. As the craft room was so small the girls pushed two tables together in the corner of the library to use for leather work. Some crafts could be carried out on the wards. In April the unit was fortunate enough to receive a supply of Plexiglas and the men were able to make articles such as picture frames, bracelets, rings, letter openers, lockets, pins and chains.

As the weather improved the Red Cross made arrangements for patients to fish in the river Severn once open season began but in May the hospital was given notice to leave Blackmore Park so very little fishing was done.

Chapter 3

Blackmore Park Site Two – 65th and 90th General Hospitals

On 19 October 1943 the 65th General Hospital arrived on Site Two of Blackmore Park. Like the 19th the 65th was an affiliated hospital. It had its beginnings in October 1940 at Duke Hospital, North Carolina when the hospital had put together a reserve unit consisting of doctors and nurses. In July 1942 the 65th was placed on active duty and sent to Fort Bragg for basic training. Here its ranks were swelled by additional army nurses and about 500 enlisted men from the 66th General Hospital at Fort Bragg.

On 1st October 1943 the unit sailed to England on the luxury liner the Queen Elizabeth. Conditions on board were not as luxurious as they had been during the ship's civilian life as it was necessary to fit in more than 15000 medical personnel.

On arrival in England the unit was commanded by Colonel Gordon A. Clapp, a veteran from the 1st World War, and was comprised of 90 doctors, 100 nurses and 500 corpsmen. Maud Hollowell Black, one of the nurses, remembers her first impressions of Site Two, Blackmore Park as being:

"...nothing more than a cow pasture sprinkled with a posse of temporary military buildings."

She also remembers hearing the German bombers overhead at night as they flew to London. The hospital had heavy black rubber curtains to fit in with blackout restrictions.

Enlisted Men's Living quarters.
(65th General Hospital Archives)

By January 1944 the hospital was on active operation, receiving and treating patients. At the beginning of January the hospital had 190 patients, this number was increased when a number of patients were evacuated by air from Northern Ireland. In February a detachment of two officers and 20 enlisted men were detailed to set up the hospital at the nearby site of Wood Farms.

Meanwhile in East Anglia the U.S. 8th Air Force was sustaining heavy casualties and President Roosevelt, whose son, Elliot, was serving there, heard that British hospitals were giving better care to Royal Air Force casualties than their American counterparts were receiving from American hospitals. Roosevelt contacted Army Surgeon General Norman T. Kirk and Air Surgeon Major General David Grant and ordered them to England to investigate the allegations.

When word of this reached General Hawley's office in London he decided to move the 65th General Hospital to the hospital site at Redgrave Park, Botesdale, Suffolk to replace the 231st Station Hospital which was currently serving there. A general hospital could provide more beds than a station hospital and also because the 65th was an affiliated hospital from Duke University

Major General Norman T. Kirk U.S.A. The Surgeon General 1 June 1943-31 May 1947. (U.S. Military Medical Archives)

Medical School and Hospital it had the reputation of having a number of highly skilled medical personnel. General Hawley felt that the 65th would come out better at an inspection.

An advance party of the 65th arrived at Redgrave Park on 10 February 1944 and the remainder of the hospital followed on March 4th. The unit arrived on the day of the 8th Air Force's first air raid on Berlin and so the hospital received 23 wounded men that night. The next morning two bombers crashed on take off at a nearby air base and severely injured survivors were received before the previous night's work had been completed.

On 11 March Roosevelt's inspection team arrived to inspect the hospital. The investigating team was pleased with what they saw and noted that here, as in the surrounding station hospitals, the 8th Air Force were receiving superior care.

The 65th General Hospital was replaced by the 90th General Hospital at Site Two. The 90th General Hospital had been activated on 30 September 1942 at Tilton General Hospital, Fort Dix, New Jersey and was commanded by Colonel Taylor. By November 1943 it consisted of 62 officers and 101 nurses. Five American Red Cross workers were also attached to the organisation.

Nurses from the 90th after training in the mud. In the centre Dorothy Newton shows off her G.I. underwear. Note on back to Dorothy's husband of 3 weeks "Now that I haven't my love to keep me warm these (Long Johns) help a little. Poor substitute but better than none." (Claire Saxon)

On 22 December 1943 the unit embarked for England on a French troop ship, the Ile de France but for an unspecified reason the unit was disembarked and returned to Camp Kilmer, New Jersey on the night of 24th December. On 1 January the 90th boarded the Queen Elizabeth along with about 20,000 other troops. She sailed through the Arctic waters near Iceland without escort as it was thought that German submarines didn't operate in these waters. The ship anchored in the Firth of Clyde where the personnel were taken ashore in smaller craft as the Queen Elizabeth was too large to dock there.

The unit then travelled to a staging camp at Oulton Park, Cheshire, by rail and arrived on 11 January 1944. The personnel were surprised that the trains had small private compartments instead of the open cars they were accustomed to in the U.S.

Charles Fletcher, Supply Sergeant with the 90th, describes the living accommodation at Oulton Park as huts that looked like a large pipe cut in half with a door in each end. Dorothy Newton describes the interior of her hut in a letter to her husband:

> *"Five double decker bunks, five folding chairs and a small stove in the center. We are supposedly ready for inspection at any moment. No more than one day's layer of mud is to be seen on anyone's shoes. The stove is our center of attraction. While in the hut we usually cluster around it with our feet on bricks we picked up around the area to make a hearth."*

Dorothy describes one inspection that the nurses were unprepared for:

> *"Everything was coming along fine until the inspector asked us for our gas masks and mess gear. Then all hell broke loose.*
>
> *Laury had scrambled eggs and bread and butter in her cup. She dumped it in an envelope but quick! He said "Greasy isn't it?" Have you used it since breakfast?" Chew was next. She pulled her cup from under the bunk. The Colonel said, "What is this?" Answer "Coffee Sir!" I come next. No questions, just "This will have to be stopped." I had my cup filled with canned fruit."*

While at Oulton Park the personnel undertook military training. Some of the officers and nurses were placed on detached service at various other hospitals and schools during this period. In February small groups of personnel were sent for orientation to Blackmore Park to work alongside the 65th General Hospital. The main part of the unit remained at Oulton Park until March when it moved to Blackmore Park.

Charles Fletcher describes his first impressions on his arrival at Blackmore Park:

> *"When I arrived at the army camp near Malvern I was very impressed with what I saw. The many farms with beautiful houses and barns located around the rolling hills made me homesick. This place looked so much like my home in North Carolina."*

Nurse Dorothy Newton, in a letter, describes the camp at Malvern as being warmer than the one at Oulton;

> *"The sun is actually shining and we can see the hills which are usually covered in mist. There's a beautiful hill*

Charles Fletcher and Sgt. Bill Grooms showing off their G.I. haircuts. (Charles Fletcher)

Charles Fletcher, Supply Sergeant with the 90th with colleagues. (Charles Fletcher)

off in the distance that Jo and I are planning on scaling shortly. We were told that we could see as far as Bristol Bay from the top. From here it looks like a huge chunk of moldy cheese. There's a little town along the foothills that looks quite inviting."

She also found the living conditions better at Malvern:

"I am now living in a long hut with 11 other girls. We have real beds and now know the luxury of sleeping in pajamas and between sheets. … Our washroom is combined into one building and is only about 10 yards from our back door. This is real luxury. We have two stoves in our hut and one is right at the foot of my bed. I'm really becoming an expert at stoking it too."

In a letter to her aunt, Dorothy describes the birdsong she would hear while on night duty:

"…the nightingales kept me company all night long. They sound just like canaries. It's delightful to walk into the dark and hear birds singing when everything else is still. We have a cuckoo bird here that practically ruins his lungs and our imagination every morning."

On 4 March the 90th began its work as a hospital and patients, property and equipment were transferred from the 65th General Hospital. An advance party of 27 officers, 17 nurses and 170 enlisted men had been stationed with the 65th for a while before the actual transfer, which helped the smooth transition between the two hospitals. As some of the personnel were already familiar with the patients and the routines there was no interruption in patient care. Twenty British civilians who were employed with the 65th also carried on their duties at the hospital. At this point the hospital had 549 patients.

Postcards sent by Dorothy Newton while based at Blackmore Park. (Claire Saxon)

The 90th found it necessary to improve some of the facilities on site. The dental section needed a brick wall built between the operating areas and laboratory benches, shelving and boxes constructed. It was also necessary to make and improve cuspidors, an electric engine, foot stools, partitions and cabinets of various types. The department prepared facilities for a dark room, running water, developing tanks and shelving as the X-Ray facilities were very basic.

The nurses' club however, did not need much refurbishment. Dorothy Newton describes it as having:

> *"…a natural fireplace- large- that was built by the unit that occupied the place before us. They also installed a bar with a brass rail and everything."*

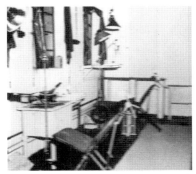

Dental surgery. (65th General Hospital Archives)

The American Red Cross unit attached to the hospital set up in one of the ward buildings which they furnished and decorated themselves. Their duties, while at Blackmore Park, were mostly in relation to the patients to whom they supplied a recreational and social service. The unit had ping pong and snooker tables, a phonograph with a good stock of records, a good stock of books and arts and craft materials. While at Blackmore Park they put on regular parties for the patients and organised entertainment from outside artists.

Nurses and Personnel from the 90th General Hospital. (Claire Saxon)

During the pre-invasion weeks groups of personnel were detached for duty in the marshalling areas. The unit particularly felt the loss when the only mess officer, half of the mess sergeants and two thirds of the cooks were sent to cater for troops in the marshalling areas.

At the end of March Dorothy had a pleasant surprise when she arrived back from a shopping trip to buy a bike in Malvern to find her husband, Clair, was waiting at the camp for her. He had been ferrying aircraft to the U.K. from Africa. The 90th gave Dorothy some leave and the couple spent a couple of days in London. On the second night:

> "...all hell let loose. It was my first air raid experience. The combined noise of the AA guns, flares and bombs dropping along with the sound of airplanes coming in waves had my heart palpitating for well over one hour. It was exciting but once will be enough ... It's a most peculiar feeling to just lie and wonder if a bomb will fall your way."

The couple parted in London on 30th March, Dorothy's birthday. Sadly it was the last they saw of each other. Clair returned to the States and Dorothy returned to Malvern. On June 7th Dorothy left England to return to the States as she was pregnant. At this time her husband, Clair, was 'flying the hump' between India and Burma. His last flight was in Burma in August 1944, at which point he was listed as 'missing'. The crash site is still to be located.

During May the unit came under the jurisdiction of the 12th Medical Center and in anticipation of D-Day in May the bed capacity of the hospital was increased to 1365 by erecting tented wards. Five days after D-Day the first train load of casualties was received from France.

The patients were unloaded at Malvern Wells Station. The archivist for the 12th Hospital Center which had responsibility for the hospitals in the Malvern area noted at the time that:

> "Some difficulty was encountered in the unloading of these casualties due to the inexpedient condition and arrangement of the station platform and adjacent features. The situation had been anticipated early in April 1944 when a survey was made by the Center Commanding Officer. On 29 April 1944 an urgent request was made for the construction and improvement of facilities for the loading and unloading of patients at Malvern Wells Railroad Station. However progression of the project was delayed and the construction of a new siding was not completed and available for use until 26 June 1944 when it was first used for the unloading of patients." (12th Hospital Center Archives)

Edward Jones, living in Great Malvern at the time remembers:

"As a young lad I watched this area being constructed by earth moving equipment the like of which I had never seen before."

Edward also remembers seeing the whole area covered with ambulances as the soldiers disembarked:

"First the walking wounded and then those on stretchers and last, stretchers with sheets over, which I assume was the poor chaps who hadn't made the journey."

Unloading hospital trains at Malvern Wells Station. (The 53rd General Hospital)

Ambulances parked on the Peachfield Road Siding at Malvern Wells Station. (The 53rd General Hospital)

He recalls that once the ambulances were full they would turn in different directions out of Peachfield Road, some uphill and some downhill, presumably taking the soldiers to the hospital with the specialism to deal with their particular injuries.

Tony Clay, also a young lad at the time, remembers playing cricket on Malvern Link Common with a group of friends when he saw a train coming with two engines and 11 coaches:

> *"Each coach had a white patch and a red cross to show it was a hospital train. I can remember looking at the chaps inside and they looked absolutely dead, they just looked straight through me. They looked completely shell shocked. We went on playing cricket and about two hours later more trains came through full of men looking completely vague. We realised later that this was after D-Day."*

Pam Drew also remembers watching the hospital trains coming in. At first she found it upsetting but she remembers that after a while the residents of Malvern became used to it. She recalls that the hospital trains had priority on the line over the civilian trains and sometimes the train she was travelling home from work on would have to wait in a siding while the hospital train went through.

From the middle of June onwards the 90th General Hospital was almost full to capacity. A large number of patients with long bone fractures were admitted and were treated by skeletal traction. There were also a large number of patients with thoracic injuries, some of which had been transferred from other hospitals of the 12th Medical Center.

As was to be expected after D-Day much of the work carried out at the hospital changed. Prior to D-Day the laboratory section had been carrying out routine laboratory work involving haematology and chemistry whereas afterwards it was necessary for the section to carry out more tests involving bacteriology due to the large influx of surgical patients.

Naturally the X-Ray Department also became busier after D-Day. The department was handicapped by the fact that all of the machines were in a single room which meant that it was necessary to stop all other work when fluoroscopy was carried out. The small number of cassettes available to the department made it

Laboratory.
(65th General Hospital Archives)

X-Ray Department.
(65th General Hospital)

necessary to stop and reload while examining a case if more than three large films were needed. Before D-Day the largest number of examinations carried out on a single day was 30. On 22 June 103 examinations were carried out.

A number of thoracic surgical cases were received after D-Day, some were transferred from other hospitals in the 12th Hospital Center. They were operated on by personnel of the Thoracic Surgery Section under the jurisdiction of Lt. Col. Arthur S. Touroff, Consultant in thoracic surgery for the 12th Hospital Center.

Prior to D-Day the Neuropsychiatric section of the hospital encountered a variety of psychiatric cases such as psychopaths, defectives, epileptics and chronic neurotics but after D-Day most patients admitted displayed symptoms of 'battle reaction', in severe cases this led to schizophrenia like reactions.

Shortly before D-Day, on 22 May 1944, the unit had been relieved from assignment to Western Base Section and assigned to Forward Echelon, Advance Section. In June the unit was alerted and prepared for movement to the continent. On 14 July there was an inspection of the hospital by General Kirk, General Hawley, Colonel Green, Colonel Lehman, C.O. of the 12th Hospital Center, Colonel Lanman and Lieutenant Colonel Cleveland.

In the last week of July the 90th left the site as the 155th General Hospital arrived. The 90th left in two echelons and turned over the base to the 155th on 29 July. During the last week of service at Blackmore Park all the nurses were replaced by those of the 155th so that the nurses of the 90th could be assigned to the 280th Station Hospital for a one week course in Tented Hospital Operation. At the time of leaving the patient census was 999. 3551 patients had been admitted during the four month period that the 90th were active at Blackmore Park Site Two.

From Blackmore Park the 90th travelled to Llandudno to await shipment to France. The nurses rejoined the unit there. On 18 August the hospital departed for a marshalling area and on 23 August arrived in France on Utah Beach. In October they set up a hospital in an old lunatic asylum at Fains les Sources.

Chapter 4
12th Hospital Center

As American forces hospitals became established in the U.K. General Paul R. Hawley, the E.T.O. Chief Surgeon intended to organise the hospitals into clusters of four or five for greater efficiency. The five hospitals in the Malvern area, two at Blackmore Park, one at Brickbarns, one at Wood Farm and one at Merebrook were to come together under the jurisdiction of the 12th Hospital Center.

A hospital center was a group of hospitals, general, station and convalescent operating under a single headquarters. Station hospitals would serve the needs of troops training in the U.K. while general hospitals would take patients wounded in action, general hospitals having the capacity of just over 1,000 beds, while station hospitals could take just over 800 patients. Convalescent hospitals would take convalescing patients from both types of hospital.

Hawley intended patients being evacuated from the continent to travel by train. Each train would carry two to three hundred patients. As patients arrived at each hospital center they could be directed to the hospital which would best deal with their injuries. Thus each hospital within a group could concentrate on a certain type of surgery or treatment. This way equipment and personnel could be concentrated where they would be most effective.

The hospitals under the jurisdiction of the 12th Hospital Center all specialised in one or more types of surgery or treatment. Site Two at Blackmore Park dealt with thoracic injuries. The 53rd at Merebrook, Hanley Swan, specialised in burns and plastic surgery, it took many of the first casualties from the D-Day landings. The 55th at Wood Farm, Malvern Wells carried out neural surgery while the 96th at Brickbarns, Malvern Wells, treated neural cases. Brickbarns had high fences to keep shell-shocked patients inside although they sometimes escaped and local people would find them walking around looking dazed and confused.

There were to be seven hospital centers in the U.K. These would be situated in Taunton, Devon; Blandford, Dorset; Devizes, Wiltshire; Cirencester, Gloucestershire; Whitchurch, Shropshire; Newmarket, Cambridgeshire and Great Malvern, Worcestershire. The 12th Hospital Center at Great Malvern was one of the largest centres. As well as American patients it was responsible for a number of French patients.

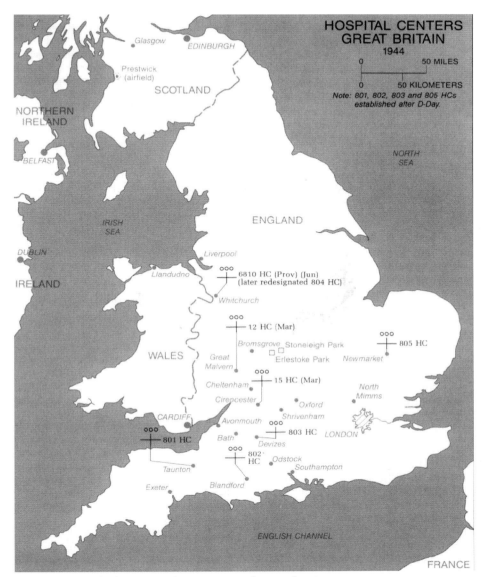

Map showing Medical Centers in the U.K. (U.S. Military archives)

The 12th Medical Center had been activated in 1942 at Camp Gruber, Oklahoma. Its mission was to:

> *"...act as a headquarters for a group of from three to ten general hospitals. Within the scope of this function was included the training of personnel in administrative supply and professional procedures, whereby attached hospitals could be relieved of administrative and*

supply details and problems by coordinating their activities, thus attention might be devoted to the improvement of professional services." (12th Hospital Center Archives)

On 27th February 1944 the unit sailed for England on the U.S.A.T. Cristobal in a convoy of about thirty ships. On 9th March, after an uneventful journey the ship docked at Swansea, Glamorganshire and the personnel disembarked and entrained for Great Malvern. On 11 March the unit began work to set up the Hospital Center at Malvern Link.

It's possible that the location of Malvern was chosen because of its proximity to the railway line. Hospital trains were able to travel from the docks at Southampton, Avonmouth and Bristol via the Great Western Railway to Great Malvern.

Diana Medley, who lived near the railway, remembers that it was said that the single line on the G.W.R. that went through the tunnel under the Malvern Hills was the busiest piece of single line in·the country during the war. Diana remembers the constant noise, day and night from the railway. Steam trains were often double headed as the gradient to the tunnel was so high.

War time train ticket. (Claire Saxon)

Various prominent buildings around Malvern Link were commandeered for use as administrative and living quarters. Many of the buildings allocated to the 12th were in a poor state of repair and unfit for living and working in so the first job of the personnel was to repair and remodel them. The shortage of vehicles for the transportation of building materials made the situation more difficult. All available personnel and equipment were assigned the task of setting the buildings in order:

"Peacetime carpenters, painters and plumbers from the organization were told what was wanted and in many instances without proper tools and equipment they set to work making necessary repairs and alterations. Showers, baths and other plumbing fixtures were installed or improved; ranges, stoves, heaters, boilers and fireplaces were repaired and put into working order; countless minor repairs were made on the buildings and premises; kitchens, offices and quarters were painted and what furniture that couldn't be obtained by virtue of the powers of persuasion was constructed with professional skill and put into use." (12th Hospital Center Archives)

The Ripples (left). Buildings in Malvern Link used by the 12th Hospital Center, 2006. (M.Collins) The Laurels (right). (M.Collins)

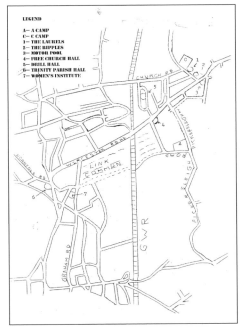

Map of Malvern Link showing buildings used by the 12th Hospital Center. (12th Hospital Center)

Colonel Lehman. (The 53rd General Hospital Archives)

By 5th April all the buildings assigned to the center had been repaired and improved and were ready for occupation. By this date all the offices had been furnished and fully equipped with the exception of the installation of telephones in the headquarters building. On 11th April two telephones were installed and on 12th April a BBx5x20 switch board was installed and on 20th April a report was submitted to headquarters, Western Base section, that the 12th Hospital Center was ready to be activated.

Colonel Asa M. Lehman with Lady Beauchamp at a garden party. (Malvern Gazette)

At Wednesday's Garden Party for the American wounded: Sir Cedric Hardwicke (who has just returned to this country from the United States), with Lady Beauchamp, the Officer-in-charge of group of American hospitals in Worcestershire, and Lady Hardwicke.

On 20th April the Commanding officer, Colonel Asa. M. Lehman received a telephone call from the Surgeon General, Western Base section, to inform him that the center would be opened on 22nd April and this was substantiated by a letter dated 22nd April and received 26th April to that effect. The 12th Hospital Center began operating as headquarters for the 19th and 90th General Hospitals at Blackmore Park, the 53rd at Merebrook, the 55th at Wood Farm and the 96th at Brickbarns from that date.

However there was some discrepancy over the opening date as on 3rd June a letter was received from Headquarters, Western Base Section, dated 30th May stating that the 12th Medical Hospital Center was officially opened as of 0001 hours, 8th May 1944. Nevertheless the difference of a fortnight in the paperwork did not affect the smooth running of the setting up at the hospital centre.

Hospitals Operating as part of the 12th Hospital Center by the end of 1944

Plant Number	Place	Number of hospital
4167	Stoneleigh	307 S.H.
4168	Bromsgrove	123 S.H.
4169	Wolverley	52 G.H.
4170	Bewdley	297 G.H.
4171	Bewdley	114 G.H.
4172	Blackmore Park	93 G.H.
4173	Blackmore Park	155 G.H.
4174	Brickbarns	96 G.H.
4175	Merebrook	53 G.H.
4176	Wood Farm	55 G.H.
4177	Leominster	135 G.H.
4178	Foxley	123 G.H.
4179	Foxley	156 G.H.
4180	Kington	122 G.H.
4181	Kington	107 G.H.
4182	Abergavenny	279 S.H.
4183	Rhyd Lafar	81 G.H.
4148	Camarthen	232 S.H.

S.H. – Station Hospital. G.H. – General Hospital.

By D-Day, 6 June 1944, all administrative duties connected with the reception and evacuation of patients were being coordinated and controlled by the Receiving and Evacuation Section of the Hospital Center.

By this time there were seven general hospitals attached to the centre, the five in the Malvern area plus the 52nd General Hospital at Wolverley and the 76th General Hospital at Leominster. The total bed capacity was 9481 of which 2055 were already filled. On 10th June 1944 the first trainload of casualties from Normandy intended for the 12th Hospital Center was unloaded at Malvern Wells station.

From the 23rd June 1944 the 5th Hospital Train Unit was officially attached to the 12th Hospital Center for permanent station duty. This unit operated two ambulance trains and two ward cars. The train unit consisted of eleven coaches, one serving as a barracks car for the enlisted personnel and one for the officers, a kitchen car, a combination office and a pharmacy car, the latter also serving as a first aid room. Ambulatory patients used car three while car four was for litter patients. The trains, which were of British design and equipment, could carry 84 patients.

Home Ambulance Train number 57 was stationed at Peachfield Siding, Malvern Wells on the Great Western Railway. The personnel from this train found it necessary to work on the limited facilities at Malvern Wells between runs. An ablutions hut was built, light and water installed and the entire site improved by further construction. At first the personnel were quartered and messed with the 12th Hospital Center but after two weeks it was decided that the unit could work more efficiently if it were billeted on the train. Although this meant that the billeting arrangements were cramped the food cooked in the train kitchens was:

> *"...excellently prepared and the cooks contribution in this line is a large factor in the contentness and high morale of the personnel. They are all unanimous in the opinion that the food is prepared better than they have had in their army careers."* (5th Hospital Train Unit)

C47 awaiting patients at Pershore Airfield. (Paul Simmons)

Ambulance and crew from the 155th General Hospital waiting to take the wounded to one of the hospitals. (Paul Simmons)

Cars number 203 and 206 were stabled on the same line at Great Malvern. The nurses on both trains were quartered and messed with the adjacent hospitals between runs.

As well as the railway the 12th Hospital Center had the use of the RAF airfield at Pershore for receiving and evacuating patients. Patients to be transported back to the U.S. would be taken by ambulance to the airfield and then transferred to C47 aircraft and usually flown to Prestwick, Scotland, or Shannon in Ireland where they would be transferred to transatlantic planes and flown to the United States.

Daniel Lennox, a staff sergeant with the 93rd, remembers transferring six critical burn patients that he had come to know well to a C47 plane that took them to Shannon Airport in Ireland. From there they were transferred to a larger transatlantic plane to return home to America. Sadly Daniel later learnt that that particular plane had gone down off the coast of Ireland.

Weather conditions would often delay flights and sometimes patients would arrive at the airfield to find that planes had been grounded. At other times there was a lack of information given to the Hospital Center regarding times of plane schedules. Both of these factors would result in patients having to be transported to and from the airfield several times before the plane actually took off. The archivist reported that:

> *"...allotments for our evacuation of patients to the Zone of the Interior often resulted in much confusion and delay."* (12th Hospital Center Archives)

There were also some delays because patients had been inadequately prepared for their journey. Examinations by medical personnel at the airfield brought to light a

Ward Tent at Pershore Airfield where interim treatment could be given. (Paul Simmons)

number of cases that had been boarded for the U.S. in a condition not sufficiently good to ensure that the trip could be made, or if it were made that it would result in harm to the patient.:

> *"...thus cases of severe anaemia, improperly applied and poorly fitting casts, infection with or without foul smelling casts, haemorrhage into a cast, pneumonia and malaria (with chills) were found, removed temporarily from the list of patients available for transfer and treated until their condition was such as to preclude anything but a normally safe journey."* (93rd General Hospital Archives)

It was necessary for corrective measures to be taken by Colonel Lehman to reduce the number of such cases.

The shortage of road transportation was also a problem for the Hospital Center throughout its time at Great Malvern. The Center had two assigned British civilian sedans which constantly needed major repair. It also had six British buses that had been allocated to the center for the use of the hospitals in its jurisdiction, which also needed constant repair work to maintain their performance. There were also British and American Radiation Laboratory vehicles which spent some considerable time in the Motor Pool being repaired. In May 1944, in readiness for D-Day casualties 65 ambulances were made available to the hospital center for the use of the hospitals. Supplemental transportation was requested and in July 1944 one sedan and one command car were added to the Motor Pool.

The 12th Hospital Center developed a reputation for high standards and it became the subject of several wartime magazine and newspaper articles. Robert Littell, freelance journalist for the Readers Digest described the Center in the following article entitled *"HOW OUR WOUNDED CAME BACK FROM NORMANDY"*:

"At evening the wounded reached the final link in the chain of their healing, at least in England. Here, in rolling open country, dozens of Nissen huts look out upon distant sheep and stone walls. This is one of half a dozen general hospitals in the area. Together they form a center where the highest medical skill is assembled from great universities and hospitals. Here specialists give each man's particular wound care that would be hard to equal in any civilian hospital.

I agree with the colonel in the medical corps who said: 'The wounded G.I. is getting a much better break than the average citizen who is hit by a car in the United States." (Readers Digest September 1944)

The Temple Telegram, a Texas newspaper, also describes the 12th Hospital Center:

"wounded fighters from France are routed within a few hours to a cluster of completely equipped hospitals in England by a United States Army Medical Center which is a key unit in the medical services smoothly moving transmission belt from the liberation front.

One of a small number of such centers organized by the Army, the unit is headed by Colonel Asa M. Lehman of Ardmore, Pennsylvania, a veteran hospital Commander with 28 years of regular army experience in two wars. Under Colonel Lehman's direction the center controls thousands of hospital beds and a large pool of ambulances available to rush patients to hospitals with plenty of bed space.

The center can handle the arrival of several hospital trains at the same time, and the huge hospitals can absorb many trainloads without having to evacuate patients to other areas. But the organization of the hospital system is designed to keep patients who have recovered from battle injuries or illnesses moving along to convalescent camps or back to military duty.

Incoming wounded men, who have already received preliminary treatment from field stations, and first aid soldiers are carefully sorted out for assignment to particular hospitals. Those with chest injuries are sent to a hospital which may also treat other types of cases but concentrates on chest wounds, burned men and men requiring plastic surgery go to another hospital, and patients requiring operations on the nerves go to still another one.

Highly specialized physicians and surgeons, experts in their fields, are shifted quickly and freely from one hospital to another for casework, diagnoses and consultations. Transfer of a physician from one hospital to another, which may be short a top notch man in some phases of medicine, is facilitated by the medical center which attempts to eliminate as much red tape as is possible.

All patients scheduled to be evacuated from the hospitals to other areas are assembled at one hospital. The hospital most conveniently located in relation to railroad stations and airfields is selected for this purpose. The medical center maintains a teleprinter connected to the Headquarters at the European Theater of Operations, trunk telephones, and a switchboard connecting all the hospitals in the cluster attached to the center.

When men are ready for transfer back to their outfits, to convalescent camps, or rest centers in the United States, the center prepares their orders and checks their records to make sure that all necessary information on their medical and military background goes with them.

Under the supervision of Colonel Lehman a special train siding has been built at the railroad station in the small English city where the medical center is located. The center plans to have a hospital train on hand at all times, if possible, and to use the siding as a base for the operation and unloading of the train." (Temple Telegram 2.07.44.)

In October 1944 the organisation of hospital centers was reviewed. On 2 October orders were issued by H.Q.U.K. Base announcing the establishment of seven provisional hospital groups in the U.K. The 5th Hospital Group was to be established with headquarters in the vicinity of Great Malvern. The Commanding Officer of the new unit was to be Colonel Lehman (C.O. of the 12th Hospital Center). On 13 October orders were sent from Headquarters U.K. Base which attached the 12th Medical Center and its assigned units to the 5th Hospital Group.

By the end of December 1944 there were 19 medical units attached to the Group and the total number of patients was 25,867. 48,936 casualties had been evacuated to the 12th Hospital Center, 16,044 of whom had been sent home to the U.S.A. as their injuries were too serious for them to be reassigned.

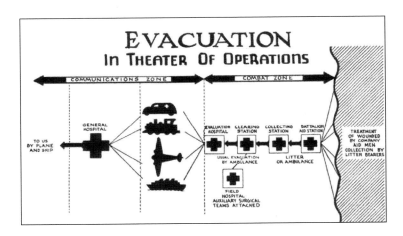

Table showing evacuation of patients. (U.S. Military Archives)

Chapter 5
93rd General Hospital

On 14 May 1944 Site One, Blackmore Park, was formally transferred from the 19th to the 93rd General Hospital. The 93rd General Hospital, commanded by Colonel Merikangus, had been activated at Fort George G. Meade, Maryland on 25 June 1943. On 20 June 1944 the hospital embarked for England aboard the H.M.S. Aquitania. The seas were particularly rough at this time of the year and Staff Sergeant Daniel Lenox remembers that the heaving seas made him feel so sick that it was difficult to walk to the dispensary for his inoculations. He finally made it on his hands and knees.

Nurse Ruth Gregg writes to her fiancé from aboard the Aquitania:

> *"At this particular point the ship is rocking and rolling with a vengeance, and so, between holding Mary pack's head and hanging on to the bunk to keep from rolling out I'll try to tell you a little bit about what's been happening. …The boat feels as though it's going to the bottom of Davy Jones locker every once in a while."* (Ruth Gregg collection)

Letter sent by Ruth Gregg to her fiance Dr. Harold Rossi. (Ruth Gregg Collection)

Nurse Ruth Gregg of the 93rd. (Ruth Gregg Collection)

Ruth was impressed with her accommodation on board as she and her fellow nurses were given a State Room and even a cockney steward. An M.P., who the girls named 'Frankie' because he sang them to sleep each night, was placed outside in the corridor.

NOTICE OF CHANGE OF ADDRESS

(A sufficient number of these cards will be distributed to each soldier when his mail address is changed to permit him to send one to each of his regular correspondents.)

Date FEB 14 1944 , 1944

This is to advise you that my correct address now is—

2nd Lt.   Gregg, Ruth M   N761819
(Grade)   (Name)   (Army Serial No.)

93rd General Hospital
(Company or comparable unit)   (Regiment or comparable unit)

APO No.   9639   % Postmaster   NEW YORK
(Strike out if not applicable)   (Name of post office)

Signature   Ruth M. Gregg

NOTE.—Newspapers and magazines may need your old address for correct processing.

My old address was   93rd General Hospital
                                          Ft. Geo. G. Meade, Md.

W. D., A. G. O. Form No. 204
April 8, 1943   Col. MenKango   16—33987-1 GPO

Notification of change of military mailing address for Ruth Gregg giving overseas A.P.O. number. Signed by C.O. of 93rd General Hospital. (Ruth Gregg Collection)

After landing at Gouroch, Scotland, on 28 February the unit proceeded to the staging hospital at Colwyn Bay. While there a detachment from the 93rd was sent to operate a station hospital in Kilrea, Londonderry, Northern Ireland from 7 April to 31 May:

> *"Although the number of patients admitted to this hospital was not great the operation served to familiarize all concerned with administrative and other procedures peculiar to this theatre."* (93rd General Hospital Archives)

On 8 May half of the unit proceeded by rail to Blackmore Park, Site One. The remainder of the unit arrived on 14 May. At the handover the 93rd exchanged 12 of their vehicles for 13 considerably older vehicles being used by the 19th. The 93rd then had the use of 22 vehicles; a staff car, two ¾ ton command cars, two ½ ton command cars, four ½ ton American field ambulances, a ¾ ton American Field Ambulance and three 2 ton British ambulances.

As well as the American medical personnel 33 British civilian workers were assigned to the hospital by the British Ministry of Labour. The women were

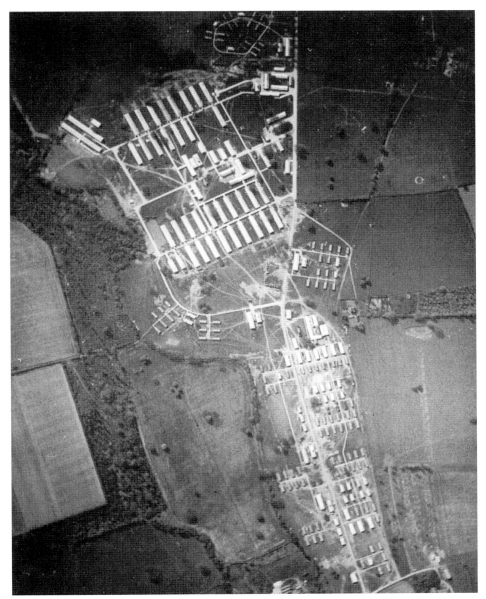

Aerial photo of the 93rd General Hospital Site One. (93rd General Hospital Archives)

employed as telephone operators, seamstresses and ward maids while the men worked on maintenance and repair of the hospital utilities.

One of the telephone operators remembers working in the telephone exchange in the headquarters block. She recalls that the switchboard looked like a giant piano. Twelve women operated the switchboard, there were 316 extensions and nine outside lines. Three lights would light up periodically, the red one was for the Commanding Officer, the green for the Adjutant and the amber one for the other personnel.

She used a bike to travel to work but one day her bike disappeared from the rack. As she worked different shifts, some late at night, an arrangement was made for a vehicle from the Motor Pool to collect her from her home and take her back again until the bike mysteriously appeared again.

Colonel Merikangus was to write about the civilian personnel in July 1945:

> *"Most of this personnel has been of very great help in view of the military personnel shortages but the main difficulty with the majority of them has been to have them understand that regularity of working hours and dependability are very important assets in a military installation."* (93rd General Hospital Archives)

Electricity for the hospital came from a British substation at Tewkesbury. On the rare occasion that there was a power cut the hospital had a British built auxiliary plant which supplied the operating theatre and six adjacent wards in emergencies. Solid fuel was supplied by the British O/C of Barracks Stores. During December, as a result of a general shortage of solid fuel in the United Kingdom there was a campaign for fuel economy and this resulted in the consumption by the 93rd being the:

> *"...lowest per capita weight of solid fuel of any installation in the Western District."* (93rd General Hospital Archives)

Water for the hospital came from a British War Department pumping station at Bromsberrow, about ten miles southeast of the hospital. The water came from a fresh water well and was chlorinated at source. A six inch cast iron main then transported the water into a reservoir at the camp built to hold 58,000 gallons. The average daily consumption of the hospital was 90,000 gallons.

Sewage was carried to a pumping station within the hospital area. This pumping station also served three other hospitals in the vicinity. From here the sewage was pumped to a sewage disposal plant three miles outside Malvern. Unfortunately the pumping station was prone to break down during and after rain storms. At these times, and whenever a power failure occurred, the sewage backed up and poured from nearby manholes where it would be diverted into a stream. Major Naegeli reported that:

> *"This, in addition to creating an unsanitary condition in the immediate vicinity of the hospital, caused pollution of the stream and is alleged to have caused the death of a number of trout therein."* (93rd General Hospital Archives)

British engineers came out several times to attempt to repair the system but without success. Plans were made to install larger pumps and to provide a diesel driven standby pump but no pumps were available. However, at the beginning of 1945, one of the manholes was elevated in order to stop the sewage overflow into the stream.

Laundry of hospital linen and personnel clothing was carried out by a civilian contractor in Birmingham. Three trips a week were made to Birmingham to collect the laundry which was processed in 72 hours. At the beginning of 1945 the linen contract was changed to a British civilian laundry in Kington, Herefordshire, which was a lot nearer. In order to supplement the laundry service the personnel were obliged to wash their own fatigue uniforms. Dry cleaning was carried out by a civilian contractor in Worcester and shoes were repaired by a civilian contractor in Hereford who repaired thirty to fifty pairs of shoes each week.

The American servicemen found the facilities in the mess halls to be poor compared to mess halls in the United States. Site One had three mess halls, one for patients, one for officers and nurses and one for enlisted men. Major Naegeli noticed that the mess personnel spent much of their time mopping and cleaning, more than would be necessary under similar conditions in America although in inspections the mess halls always received a superior rating and there were no outbreaks of gastro-intestinal disease among the personnel eating in any of the mess halls.

Daniel Lenox remembers the food prepared in the mess halls as being less than appetising and that:

> *"...whenever mutton was prepared the aroma throughout the hospital was so bad the story was told that flies flew away in the opposite direction."*

However personnel were not allowed to waste food. Plate garbage was checked at every meal to see that no edible food was wasted. The programme of reducing food wastage was:

> *"...greatly enhanced by the arrival at this hospital of several recovered American Prisoners of War who were in various degrees of starvation and who could show the most critical and particular individual that no food must be wasted."* (93rd General Hospital Archives)

Grease boxes and other items containing critical materials were salvaged by the Mess Department and turned over to British and American salvage depots. Colonel Merikangus commented that:

> *"The British people have impressed most of the Americans to how far the salvage program can be carried and as to how valuable and*

worthwhile it can be. Consequently very few items escape selection for the salvage depots from the normal general and medical supply sections as well as the last screening being done at the post incinerator." (93rd General Hospital Archives)

When the 93rd took over the hospital they also took over the existing patients. Fortunately the operating rooms were in good condition and so the surgical staff could start work straight away. The 93rd were also grateful for the number of cabinets and other furnishings built and improvised by the 19th General Hospital before them. The archivist states that the 93rd:

"...considered itself extremely fortunate to have taken over such a well stocked and equipped installation." (93rd General Hospital Archives)

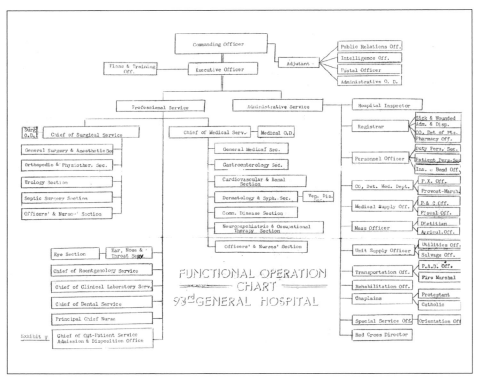

(93rd General Hospital Archives)

Ruth Gregg' first impressions of the site at Blackmore Park were that:

"...the whole place was a mess and so everything had to be straightened out, windows washed, grounds cleared up." (Ruth Gregg Collection)

Ruth was billeted in a nissen hut which she described as:

"half of a great big tin can turned upside down." (Ruth Gregg Collection)

…with five other nurses. In an attempt to make the hut look less drab the girls cut out pictures from magazines to decorate the walls and ceiling. The girls also put up a large map of France so that they could follow the progress of the war.

Collage of pictures from the 93rd General Hospital. (93rd General Hospital Archives)

Main Gate to Site One. (93rd General Hospital Archives)

In the period before D-Day Ruth Greg assisted with several operations until one day she was asked to give anaesthesia when things were busy. After this she started her training in giving anaesthesia. She was pleased to think she had acquired a new skill and enjoyed her work until she witnessed a patient die under anaesthesia. He was in the operating theatre to drain a large parapharygeal abscess. In a letter to her fiancé she describes how she felt:

> *"Those twenty minutes seemed like as many hours and for a long time afterwards we kept asking ourselves what else we could possibly have done for the boy. ... If you only could have known that awful sinking feeling when we watched that boy die under our very eyes ... nothing was of any use. He just never breathed again."* (Ruth Gregg Collection)

During 1944 there were seven other deaths at the hospital, three were battle casualties, three had medical diseases such as tuberculosis and one had a pulmonary embolism following accidental wounding in France. In 1945 there were just two deaths at the hospital, one of a patient who had developed an infection in a wound and one who had hepatitis.

The death due to anaesthesia happened on 5th June 1944. The next day was to bring an event that would bring a large influx of patients to the hospital. When Ruth Gregg heard the news about D-Day on 6th June she wrote:

> *"Now that the tension of waiting, waiting is over we can all get to work twice as hard and keep our fingers crossed as to the outcome of the fighting. ... As from today we'll be busy with a capital B."* (Ruth Gregg Collection)

On 13th June 300 D-Day casualties arrived at Blackmore Park Site One. Ruth found the sight of the first patients more harrowing than she had anticipated. She wrote to her fiancé:

> *"How can anyone ever complain or wish they were off duty when you watch those boys coming into the operating room, not uttering a single complaint but rather praising you for working so hard. It really gets you inside."* (Ruth Gregg Collection)

She found the stories individual soldiers told her even more harrowing:

"One boy was telling me about how he was wounded just as his company started retreating and so he had his buddies take him into a French peasant's home. A little old Frenchman sat up with him all that night until the next day when the Germans were beaten back and the medics could get to him. The Frenchman had no medical supplies of any kind but his wife made him some tea and they poured some of their hoarded rum into it and gave it to the kid." (Ruth Gregg Collection)

She was also upset when a young lieutenant came in who had recently married a nurse stationed in England:

"He had a bad leg injury and knew that there was that awful question of amputation. He prayed before he went in that he would either die on the table or his leg would be saved. It was amputation and now we have a greater problem in his mental attitude than we ever had with his physical condition." (Ruth Gregg Collection)

She admits:

"I thought I knew what these days would be like – it's easy to talk about the various types of cases you're going to have – but somehow you don't quite seem to wake up in the realisation of the facts until you are actually in the middle of the storm." (Ruth Gregg Collection)

On numerous occasions following the reception of trainloads of casualties (up to 300 litter patients) as many as 50 operations per day were carried out by the six operating teams in the surgical suite. This was in addition to the work done by the Orthopaedic Section.

Many of the wounded G.I.s arriving at the hospital were very young. Jim Bain was only 19 when he was injured in Germany on 26 February 1945. Jim had originally enrolled in the Army Specialised Training Program (A.S.T.P.) while he was still at school. After he had finished high school he was sent to New York to begin a two year intensive program in engineering. Unfortunately due to the high casualties in the North Africa Campaign the army needed replacement infantry men and so, after being involved in the program for only one semester, Jim found that the A.S.T.P. was ended and he was sent for basic infantry training.

In February 1944 Jim was assigned to the 87th Infantry Division where he trained as a machine gunner and in October he was sent overseas. In December he arrived at LeHavre and became involved in the Battle of the Bulge. After 72 days of fierce fighting through France and Belgium, and after losing many of his comrades Jim

Jim Bain (left) with Gunners Assistant Ray Denton. (Jim Bain)

arrived at the German border where his unit were given the objective to secure the town of Auw and then move on to the towns of Olzheim and Neuendorf. Jim recalls:

"We were dug in using the ruins of a blown out farmhouse in Auw. The whole top of the building had been blown off. I don't know whose artillery had done it, but we were fighting from the rubble and attempting to capture a pillbox. I stood and ran for a better position. All of a sudden, the next thing I knew my rifle flew out of my hand and I was falling to the ground. Everything seemed to happen in slow motion. … I had been shot. I think I was hit by shells from an Automatic German weapon because as I was running, all of a sudden in my mind's eye, I saw splinters of my rifle flying through the air and falling into the snow. Several bullets hit my rifle but only one went into my left forearm. The bullet hit my bone and opened up quite a hole as it exited. … I crawled and walked a couple of hundred yards back until I saw a medic who pointed me to the aid station."

Here Jim was given an injection and taken by ambulance to another station. Eventually he ended up at a tented hospital. During Jim's 72 days of fighting he had only had the chance to shower and change into clean clothes once. When the medical staff cut away his clothes which included two layers of underwear and two sets of trousers, a quantity of dead skin and hair came away with the clothes. Jim was surprised that once the ward boy had removed his boots several medical staff came to inspect his feet. He was unaware that he had contracted trench foot. When his boots were removed his feet swelled up and there was some concern that he would lose parts of his feet. Because of the nature of his injuries he was given his first aeroplane ride. He flew by C47 to England along with about twenty stretcher cases and a number of casualties that could sit up. Jim arrived at the 93rd in March. After a few weeks at the hospital he was relieved to find that amputation of his feet would be unnecessary. He recalls:

"All I know is that I was really lucky. If my feet had been black instead of gray, I would have lost them."

Pencil sketch of Jim Bain drawn while at the 93rd General Hospital. (Jim Bain)

Jim recalls that evenings on the ward could be depressing:

"At night, at any given time, with 80 to 100 wounded men in the ward, you could hear crying. Men were coming to terms with personal tragedy. The young man in the cot next to me was one of them. He had been a commercial artist before the war. He lost his right forearm in combat. He wouldn't talk to anybody. … At some point during our stay, he overheard the doctors telling me that my arm was repairable and that I would not be losing my forearm. I was lucky. With that he rolled over and congratulated me and we started talking. He told me how devastated he was now that his career was ruined and how prospects for his future looked pretty bleak."

Jim asked him if he would sketch him. One of the English volunteers on the ward gave him some paper, which she managed to find, even though it was very coarse.

"That young man did a sketch of me with his left hand that I could not believe. It was exactly what I looked like. … I think it even amazed him.

11. On what date does the insured allege that continuous total disability caused him to cease work, or if in military or naval service, he relieved from duty? **26 Feb 1945**

12. What disease or injury caused the insured to be totally disabled? Wd, lac, antero-lateral aspect mid-forearm lt, Paralysis of nerve, left radial, partial, secondary to #1

13. Places and dates of residence of insured since the date on which the alleged total disability began, and for 2 years prior thereto—
Street and No. or R. F. D.   Post office   State   Date

U.S. Army Hospital

14. Names and addresses of hospitals at which the insured has been treated—

Name Address	Date of admission	Date of release
109th Evac Hosp, APO 403, Belgium	27 Feb 45	1 Mar 45
34th Med Bn, (Prov Hosp) APO 403	1 Mar 45	21 Mar 45
28th Field Hosp Y 33, France	21 Mar 45	21 Mar 45
34th Gen Hosp, Plant 4125, APO 519	21 Mar 45	22 Mar 45
93rd Gen Hosp, Plant 4172, APO 121	22 Mar 45	4 May 45
825 Conv Cntr Plant 4123, UK	4 May 45	18 May 45
55th Gen Hosp, Plant 4176, England	18 May 45	28 May 45 (a) ove:

15. Give names and addresses of all doctors who have attended the insured for the disease or injury causing continuous total disability (except doctors who may have treated the insured only while both the insured and the doctors were in the military or naval service). Also date of treatment. If insured has been examined or treated by a private physician, or physicians, during the past year submit a supplemental statement by such physician, or physicians, under oath, preferably on the physician's letterhead, showing length of time under treatment, history of condition, physical and laboratory findings, diagnosis and prognosis, and any other pertinent medical data relating to the insured's condition.

U.S. Army Doctors

Medical form listing Jim's injuries and hospitals attended. (Jim Bain)

This was the best therapy that the young artist could have had. After spending a short time at a nearby convalescent hospital Jim was released to return home from the 55th General Hospital at Wood Farm in May 1945 and sailed from Southampton on the hospital ship SS Argentina.

Because of the large number of casualties, Wardmaster, Staff Sergeant Daniel Lenox sometimes found it necessary to work 39 hours straight through at critical times. He was often involved in taking blood, giving plasma, and stitching wounds. He remembers caring for a very lucky patient who had been shot in the left temple:

> "The bullet came through the roof of his mouth and stopped on his tongue. The doctors, nurses and I watched the swelling on his tongue to make sure his throat did not stop the air from getting to his lungs. Luckily the bullet did not harm his brain, also he never lost any teeth. He said when the incident happened he spit the bullet out on the ground."

Daniel had a lot of respect for most of the doctors he worked with but not for the one who attempted to send a limping G.I. back to the front. When Colonel Merikangus saw the G.I. he ordered that tests be carried out and it was found that a wooden bullet was lodged in the wounded man's hip. Wooden bullets had been outlawed but here was evidence that the German forces were still using them.

Other soldiers would go to great lengths to avoid returning to the front line. Daniel remembers one man who feigned insanity by repeatedly sticking his head inside a soiled laundry box and three other men who admitted to shooting themselves in the foot.

As soon as the 93rd had arrived at Blackmore Park it had instituted a rehabilitation training programme for all classes of patients. This included intensive rehabilitation exercises, lectures and demonstrations prior to returning to the combat zone. This continued until 1 December 1944 when the hospital was expanded to 1600 beds.

The hospital was originally expanded on June 25 1944 by the erection of hospital ward tents on cement block floors at the rear of 25 of the 35 wards. This increased the capacity by a third to 1,459. During November all hospital tents were winterized by the construction of interior side walls of beaver board and the hinged doors at either end. Also at this time five officers from the Medical Service were assigned temporarily to the Surgical Service because of the increase in surgical patients to the hospital. By December it was found that even this provision was inadequate so two additional beds were put in each ward. Some of the less used rooms were converted into temporary wards and some wards into double deckered wards by using bunk beds. This brought the capacity of the hospital up to 1609.

At this point the part of the hospital used for rehabilitation was converted into two wards for the treatment of orthopaedic battle casualties and the rehabilitation Section was temporarily closed. From this date forward all class A and B patients were transferred directly to designated rehabilitation or reconditioning hospitals elsewhere in the United Kingdom. The rehabilitation programme for class C and D (bed and convalescent) patients continued.

The orthopaedic clinic had been set up soon after D-Day because of the large proportion of orthopaedic injuries among the battle casualties. The clinic was set up and equipped with its operating theatres and an X-ray unit with developing room. Using a room just for orthopaedic injuries removed the cleaning problem associated with the extensive use of plaster of paris. These arrangements enabled the orthopaedic section to see and treat more than twice the number of patients with less time wasted.

Until the beginning of 1945 it was the policy to send patients with trench foot back to the United States for treatment as it was thought they could not be rehabilitated. When it was found that it was possible to rehabilitate patients with trench foot a rehabilitation section was re-established in the hospital. On 29th February 1945 two medical wards filled with double deckered bunks and two ward tents were set aside for the use of the rehabilitation department which consisted of 2nd Lieutenant Gene Innocenti, who had previous training in rehabilitation and three men, two of whom had been trained in rehabilitation work at the 307th Station Hospital. A medical officer was assigned to supervise the medical aspects of the programme and the disposition of the patients. The wards accommodated 160 patients. Among the rehabilitation patients were five officers and several non-commissioned offices that were willing to assist in the administration of the programme.

At first morale was low on the rehabilitation wards as they were filled with the men who had thought that their condition gave them a ticket back to the U.S. and it was necessary for the Red Cross workers to have short interviews with these patients to help them make the adjustment to the fact that many of them were not going home yet.

"However they rapidly accustomed themselves to the military aspects of the programme. This was aided by a fairly liberal pass policy and comparative freedom from details outside their own wards." (93rd General Hospital Archives)

Of the 287 patients participating in the programme between 20 February and 8 May 1945 107 were returned to general assignment duty, 147 were returned to limited assignment duty (i.e. non combatant duties) and the remaining 33 were returned to the U.S.

During 1945 the hospital went through a number of changes. As the Allied troops pushed into Germany a number of Prisoner of War camps were liberated and the chief of the cardiovascular renal section, Major Samuel H. Schwartz was sent to spend two months on detached service at the Prisoner of War hospital with the Headquarters of the 7th U.S. Army. Many of the prisoners were in need of specialist medical attention, malnutrition being the main ailment, a large number were sent to hospitals in England. Those sent to the 93rd responded well to nutritional treatment. Three of the four patients were found to have pharyngeal diphtheria but were treated without fatalities.

V.E. Day on 8th May 1945 could not be celebrated by many of the personnel of the 93rd because of the high number of patients in the hospital although some personnel had the opportunity for passes, furloughs and leaves towards the end of May and beginning of June. Shortly after V.E. Day one of the main officer convalescent hospitals closed and as many of the patients were not yet fit, a large number were sent to the 93rd before they were evacuated back to the U.S. The large influx of 180 officer patients caused a problem at first but the mess department expanded its facilities and a portion of the duty Officers' Club was set aside for the convalescent patients as a day room.

A number of officers and enlisted men from the 93rd were reassigned during March 1945. New medical officers were sent as replacements but they were often found to be under-qualified. Replacements were also sent for the enlisted personnel but many of the replacements were soldiers who had been placed on limited assignment after having spent time in one of the hospitals. It was necessary to return a number of the replacements to the U.S. as they were not physically fit enough to be working in a hospital.

The change of personnel made it difficult for the hospital to function as efficiently. Colonel Merikangus wrote:

> "We realize the immense problems involved in redeployment of units and reassignment of personnel as individuals but the problem is also a trying one for this unit which is still taking care of over 500 patients while all this turnover of officer and enlisted personnel is taking place. … At the present we have approximately one-third of our original nursing staff and we have no replacements for some of the transferred nurses and most of the replacements we have received are here only on a temporary duty status from a nearby closing general hospital." (93rd General Hospital Archives)

In June Detachment A, commanded by Colonel Richard B. Warriner, was transferred for permanent station to Lichfield, Staffordshire. At this location the detachment was to operate a 215 bed station hospital at Plant 4185. By the end of June 1945 only one third of the original nursing staff remained.

For a time it was thought that the shortage of enlisted personnel could be balanced by the use of German Prisoners of War for various utilities and outside details and also in the mess halls but the project was abandoned by higher headquarters before any prisoners of war could be utilised. Colonel Merikangus commented:

> "*In order to make up for the shortage in numbers of personnel the remaining men did everything in their power to cover and to work that much more diligently. Also we were required to use as many ambulant patients as possible on a semi-duty status in order to take care of the very large area of this hospital and to keep up the proper maintenance and repair.*" (93rd General Hospital Archives)

In July 1945 orders were received for the 93rd General Hospital to be closed and the site to be turned over to the British authorities. A conference was arranged with the British Ministry of Works and all materials belonging to their office were carefully checked and returned. The supplies which the 93rd thought they would need to function at their new site were packed and sent to Shugborough Park, Staffordshire. During the last week of July the entire patient population was sent back to the U.S. with the exception of about twenty who were transferred to the 53rd General Hospital at Merebrook.

On 25 August the hospital received orders to separate. The Headquarters unit was to proceed immediately to the site of the 67th General Hospital at Blackburn Park (Fairford) Detachment A were to remain at their present site in Lichfield Staffordshire.

On 17th September orders came stating that both Headquarters and its detachment were to cease operations in the U.K. and to proceed to a staging area for return to the United States. Detachment A was to hand over to Detachment A of the 347th Station Hospital while the Headquarters unit was to hand over to the Headquarters unit of the 231st station hospital which had spent the previous few weeks in Malvern Wells. Colonel Merikangus completes his report for 1945 by stating:

> "*I personally feel very proud of the efforts and accomplishment of this organisation and believe that each and every officer, nurse, enlisted man, Red Cross worker and civilian employee has worked as a highly cooperative and homogenous group to successfully fulfil the mission we were given in this conflict in the European Theatre of Operations.*" (93rd General Hospital Archives)

Chapter 6

93rd General Hospital – Special Service Section and Red Cross Unit

The Red Cross unit and the Special Service Section of the 93rd General Hospital worked together to look after the morale of the personnel and patients as well as provide entertainment for off duty time. The hospital also had two chaplains, Catholic and Protestant to look after the spiritual welfare of the personnel. They held religious services, made numerous hospital visits and wrote letters of condolence to relatives of seriously ill battle casualties. In 1944 it was necessary for the Protestant chaplain to hold services for people of the Jewish faith as no Jewish chaplain was available. In 1945 a Jewish chaplain, Chaplain Grossman, was attached to the Headquarters of the 12th Hospital Center and he was able to make frequent visits to Jewish personnel. When the Jewish chaplain arrived a dinner was given by the other chaplains of the 12th Medical Center. Bishop Henry Knox Sherrill, Bishop of the Diocese of Massachusetts, who was touring England at the time, also attended the dinner.

The Special Service officer, 1st Lieutenant Thomas F. Mitchell and his staff took care of subscriptions to army publications such as Yank and Stars and Stripes, provided speakers and information for the weekly orientation talks, provided facilities and equipment for various recreational activities and games, made

Bishop Henry Knox Sherrill of the diocese of mass., U.S.A., with Chaplain Charles Lovin, chief chaplain of the 12th U.S. Medical Center, Chaplain Grossmann and Chaplain Oran C. Zaeibst (the bishop's aide-de-camp) at a dinner held at the Westminster Arms Hotel West Malvern on Thursday week. (Malvern Gazette)

Stars and Stripes and Yank. (Authors Collection)

reservations for personnel going on leave and furlough and put on movies most evenings. The British Ministry of Information worked in cooperation with the Special Service Section and provided several speakers for talks such as the one on the Japanese by Samuel Sokobin, the American Consul in Birmingham.

A public address system was installed in the hospital by the Special Service so that bed patients could listen to shows even if they were unable to get to the Recreation Hall. During the day and early evening the Armed Forces Network and similar radio stations were broadcast throughout the system to all wards. Occasionally loudspeakers were turned off in a particular ward if it was thought inadvisable for patients on that ward to listen to particular programmes.

The Special Service also organised sports activities such as softball and volleyball. Colonel Merikangus was of the opinion that:

> *This had provided a very wholesome outlet for the sports fever which every true American feels, both for the participants and the spectators."*
> (93rd General Hospital Archives)

For rainy days the Special Service provided snooker and table tennis tables in the enlisted men's recreation building, the N.C.O. club, the Red Cross building and the Officers' Club.

In addition to the sports fixtures the Special Service arranged for weekly trips to the Shakespeare Memorial Theatre in Stratford on Avon. Plays by Shakespeare and other playwrights were presented nightly. Trips were also arranged to dances and concerts held in nearby cities.

Colonel Merikangus had requested a Red Cross Unit be attached to the 93rd while still at Fort George G. Meade in Maryland and a group of six girls were sent. They assumed their duties at Blackmore Park on May 12 1944 and they continued where the Red Cross unit attached to the 19th had left off.

Norah Duffy, the Assistant Field Director arranged a programme for the patients so that each ward had either crafts or entertainments once a week. She requested that each ward nurse should furnish one patient each to help with collecting

Chart showing organisation of Red Cross Units. (19th General Hospital Red Cross Archives)

supplies, assist with games and to generally act as liaison officer between the Red Cross and the ward. The drawback with the system was the frequent change of personnel in the wards. Because after D-Day the hospital was mainly dealing with battle casualties, the Red Cross felt that activities should be centred around the ward as a large number of patients were confined to the ward.

As new patients arrived at the hospital the Red Cross distributed cigarettes and gum and then served hot chocolate on the ward. This gave the girls the opportunity to speak to the patients, answer their questions and take their requests. As the frequency of patients arriving at the hospitals increased, many of the patients were arriving in the early hours of the morning so the girls devised a system where they visited the men later in the morning after they had had the chance to sleep.

The girls would also be expected to see the patients off at the train station when they left the hospital. It was the policy to give each man a ditty bag holding candy, gum and cigarettes. By October 1944 the large influx of patients from the Battle of the Bulge had brought the cigarette stocks low so instead of giving each man a packet, an open box was passed among the men to take one cigarette each. The girls also gave out back issues of Life magazine and current copies of Stars and Stripes for the men to read on the train. By December stocks of ditty bags were also low.

Letter writing and conversation were the main services that the men required. One of the recreation workers even found it necessary to run a lip reading class each week because of a number of patients arriving who had become deaf.

Many of the patients had social problems for the Red Cross to deal with but due to the short stay of each patient it was difficult to deal properly with many of the problems. There were many requests to locate relatives and friends so Charlotte Stuart, the secretary, would spend much of her time on the phone. The Red Cross also received requests from the U.S. regarding the welfare of some of the patients. The girls were not allowed to answer these requests until halfway through July 1944 when security restrictions were relaxed. Many of the requests were difficult to deal with because the patient had been transferred, returned to duty or started their journey back to the U.S.

Craft work was popular at the 93rd. Many of the patients awaiting transportation home were keen to make presents like cuddly toys to give to their families when they were reunited with them. The craft section was also able to provide materials and instructions to bed patients and severely handicapped ambulatory patients on the ward. In October 1944 the Red Cross put on a craft exhibition in Malvern, in which the towns people were, 'exceedingly interested'. In December the Red Cross had a stall at a large two day county fair for the benefit of St. John Ambulance and the British Red Cross. Red Cross units in the nearby hospitals also participated and it was considered to be a great success.

To supplement the Red Cross activities, around twelve British WVS workers volunteered for duty in the Red Cross building and among the wards. Two of the ladies were chosen to be 'Grey Ladies' and were on duty two days a week. Prior to working at the hospital the women were given an orientation lecture in order to go over security and other issues. The WVS supported the hospital in other ways. They sent flowers to put in the wards and did shopping for the personnel and patients. Tours and parties were organised and a 'Welcome Club' for servicemen was opened by the WVS in Malvern. Colonel Merikangus valued the work the WVS did for the hospital and wrote in his report:

"These women have been of invaluable assistance to our Red Cross workers and they, we believe, have also enjoyed the privilege of working with our fine fighting men." (93rd General Hospital Archives)

As a gesture of appreciation a tea was laid on for the ladies at Broadway in Worcestershire.

The WVS were also able to help when the Red Cross organised dances on the post by selecting girls and chaperones to attend as they had for the 19th General Hospital. Colonel Merikangus was so pleased with the success of the first dance organised in September 1944 for the rehabilitation patients that he asked the Red Cross to organise one each month.

In November 1944 it was necessary for the girls to plan ahead for Christmas. A number of personnel met with the Red Cross in the Red Cross building prior to Christmas to tie packages and make decorations for wards where patients were unable to make their own. The mess halls were all decorated and the Red Cross building was decorated with greenery. Silver stars were cut from tin cans to decorate the tree.

Two trees were ordered for each ward and Red Cross supplies such as patterns, paste string and glue were distributed between the wards. One of the officer patients donated two war saving bonds as prizes for the most original and attractive wards. There was great secrecy regarding the decorations, two wards even put up pre-Christmas decorations as a hoax. The wards were judged on 23rd December by the Chief Nurse of the 12th Hospital Center, Lieutenant Colonel

Rousch, Major Bacaira of the 96th General Hospital and Major Acock of the 155th General Hospital. The winning ward had a blue and white colour scheme, the tree being white with blue stars and real Christmas lights. The second prize was given to a ward that had a small Santa Claus parachuting out of a bomber over a Christmas tree.

On Christmas Day two Santa Clauses and a Sad Sack visited each patient with a Red Cross worker. The Red Cross boxes sent from the states were given to patients as well as tartan stockings filled with oranges, raisins, candy and a small present which had been tied to their beds on Christmas Eve after the patients had gone to sleep.

Over the Christmas period the Red Cross arranged for each ward to have some form of outside entertainment. Three groups of carollers covered the entire hospital and the patients watched shows by a children's dancing class a children's pantomime and puppet show and U.S.O. and Red Cross shows.

On Christmas night the Red Cross gave a cabaret party for the entire hospital in the Recreation hall. Two shows were given, the first for the patients and the second for the hospital personnel. The hall was decorated to represent a cabaret with red gingham table cloths and bottles with candles in them on the tables. Boxes were used for seating. The show had been written by the junior recreation worker, Constance King, with the help of patient talent. Five nurses dressed as cigarette girls passed out cigarettes during the performance and enlisted men dressed in white coats acted as waiters giving out cider and crisps.

In February 1945 the hospital received an unexpected visit from H.R.H. the Princess Royal, Princess Mary who was accompanied by Miss S. Kenyen Slaney and Lady Beauchamp who had arranged the visit. She toured the hospital stopping at the Cola Bar, newly installed in the Post Exchange building where she had her first drink of cola. She also had a lunch of tomato cocktail, fried steak and iced cake in the officers mess.

The Princess Royal was able to speak knowledgeably to doctors and nurses at the hospital as she herself had had nurse training. She spoke to a number of staff and patients. She joked with one of the patients Captain Truman, telling him he looked like the Statue of Liberty with his arm in traction. She showed an interest in the patients' photos of their loved ones and also crafts they were working on. She even gave an autograph to a paratrooper who had been wounded in Belgium:

> "'I would not lose that for anything' he commented as he showed envious friends the name 'Mary' written in pencil on a small notebook." (Malvern Gazette 17/2/1945)

Another special occasion in February for the hospital was the hospitals first anniversary overseas. To celebrate this on 28 February there was a special anniversary dinner with highly decorated cakes and an anniversary show presented by a cast of officers, nurses and enlisted men of the organisation under the supervision of Staff Sergeant Theodore D. Goldens. A souvenir roster year book was printed and distributed to each member of the organisation.

THE Princess Royal leaving a hospital with the C.O. Colonel Wayne Brandstadt and Colonel Lehmann Colonel Merikangus.

Malvern Gazette 17/2/1945.

In July 1945 the Red Cross had a new Assistant Field Director, Rose Daniels. At this point the hospital had only 350 patients so she decided to shift the emphasis of the Red Cross work. She introduced afternoon trips for ambulatory patients where the patients could take part in golfing, horseback riding, swimming and tennis. In Malvern an officer or enlisted men was put in charge of each group of patients and a Red Cross worker accompanied the largest group. The men would be dropped off in Malvern and picked up a few hours later,

When the patient population was sent back to the U.S. the girls ensured that the patients had everything they would need for their trip back home and then set about making inventories of their equipment and crating everything ready for shipment to the Red Cross warehouse.

When they left Blackmore Park the girls decided to split the Red Cross unit between detachment A in Lichfield and the Headquarters detachment at Blackburn Park, Fairford. Each hospital had around 200 patients and Colonel Merikangus felt that both should have Red Cross coverage. He arranged transport so that the Assistance Field Director could visit Detachment A weekly as well as contacting them by phone daily.

Now that they were working with a smaller number of patients the girls found that they could get to know the patients better. They discussed planned group entertainment for the men and did organise some tea dances but:

"It was found that the men preferred to carry though individual plans and to relax in the more home like atmosphere which could be developed with fewer patients to plan for." (93rd General Hospital Red Cross Archives)

Pages of the anniversary booklet produced in February 1945. (93rd General Hospital Archives)

As regards case work it was possible to give longer and more complete interviews to patients and detachment men with problems, one of the problems was the uncertainty of when they would be sent home.

> *"The point of greatest need was the unrest and pressure regarding going home. It demanded even greater still and resourcefulness, especially since the Red Cross Staff could very easily find itself identifying with those men. The resilience of the young men made it possible for them to accept their situation easier."* (93rd General Hospital Red Cross Archives)

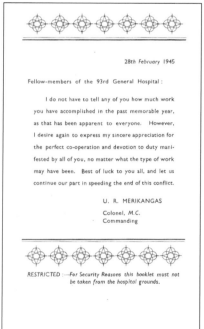

On 17 September the girls were given orders to proceed to Blandford, Dorset where they would receive orders for their return to the United States except Assistant Field Director, Rose Daniels, who would proceed to London for assignment to the Continent.

Chapter 7
155th General Hospital

The 155th General Hospital assumed operations at Blackmore Park Site Two on 29 July 1944. The 155th had been designated from the 339th Station Hospital on 23 December 1943 at Camp Ellis, Illinois. The Commanding Officer was Colonel Harry B. Gantt, a veteran of World War 1. On 23 February 1944 the unit, with a strength of 19 officers and 460 enlisted men, moved to Louisville, Kentucky. By 1 June a full complement of 56 officers, 1 Warrant Officer, 83 nurses, 3 Hospital Dieticians, 2 Physical Therapy Aides and 493 enlisted men were assigned to the unit.

An advance detachment of two officers and three enlisted men of the 155th sailed from the New York Port of Embarkation on 29 May for Glasgow on the U.S.S. America and arrived on D-Day, 6th June. The rest of the unit departed from Boston Port of Embarkation on June 26, arriving in Colwyn Bay on 4 July. They were billeted in private homes in Colwyn Bay while awaiting assignment to Blackmore Park to replace the 90th General Hospital.

Five officers, 46 nurses and dieticians and Red Cross workers arrived on Site One, Blackmore Park on 14th July while the remainder of the group arrived on 29 July. It was necessary for some of the enlisted men to be temporarily quartered in tents until the personnel of the 90th left the site.

Aeriel view of the 155th General Hospital. (English Heritage. NMR RAF Photography)

Nurses of the 155th General Hospital outside their quarters. (Battleship Cove Museum)

Nissen huts and hospital buildings of the 155th. (Battleship Cove Museum)

The nurses' quarters were sited adjacent to the hospital while the officers' quarters were located about one and a half miles away. When the 90th left, the enlisted men were billeted in huts near a farm building about half a mile from the hospital. Staff Sergeant Walter Lochbaum describes the living quarters as:

> *"...metal half moon shaped structures. On first arrival mattresses for enlisted personnel were made from a mattress cover stuffed with straw. Heat was provided by coke fired small round stoves. The Quonset hut housed six men with two tiered bunks."*

Enlisted men's billets. (155th General Hospital Archives)

Enlisted Men's Quarters, 155th General Hospital.
(Bob Elgin)

Group shot of 155th personnel outside enlisted
men's quarters. Back row: Wally James, Borge
Hansen, Bob Elgin, Jack Reiter, Les Marks.
Front Row: Pete Bisgear, Joe Brouder, Nathan
Calhoun, Joe Gearity. (Photo: Bob Elgin)

Sgt Bill Lochbaum with English bikes. (Walter Lochbaum)

Pfc Paul Simmons recalls having to walk or cycle down a narrow lane through
a farmyard, trying to avoid the cowpats, to get to the hospital. Bob Elgin
remembers that the bend in the road was given the title 'cow shit curve!' He recalls
that one of the men had a motor cycle and trying to help out the farmer, rounded
up the cows with it. Unfortunately after this experience the cows didn't give milk
for two days.

On arrival at the hospital immediate steps were taken to improve the appearance
and sanitation of the hospital area. Piles of concrete posts and building materials

Jesse Barouche sitting inside enlisted men's barracks. (Walter Lochbaum)

that were lying around were hauled away and stacked in piles for future use and stagnant pools were filled with earth. A concrete walkway was built to and around the flagpole and upright bicycle racks were replaced by stands set into the ground. Interiors of several buildings were repainted and new name plates were set up in all the wards, clinics and administration buildings. An incinerator was constructed and a steam pipe was installed near the garbage rack of the patients' mess for sterilisation of garbage cans. At the detachment mess a roofed concrete

Bend in the road enlisted men cycled down on their way to the hospital. (Paul Simmons)

Main gate of hospital. (155th General Hospital Archives)   *Main Gate 2006. (M.Collins)*

platform to house two batteries of three cans each was constructed for washing mess gear. The drain for this platform led directly into the sewer. British engineers resurfaced the tarmac road connecting the hospital and detachment area. The covered ramp system joining the east and west wings of the hospital and leading to the mess hall was completed.

This hospital also had problems with sewage which was pumped by means of a booster pump to the sewage pumping station on Site One. When there was a power cut the sewage backed up in the pipes and it was necessary to use the fire truck pump to prevent surface water and sewage from flooding the latrines, pump house motor and boiler plant. It was recommended that the hospital should have a gas or diesel powered generator with sufficient capacity to carry the entire hospital load. Unfortunately there were no stand by generators available so it was necessary for the hospital to continue to use the fire truck pump.

The hospital had the use of 26 vehicles including three British ambulances that had been adapted for the use of American type stretchers. Due to the acute rubber shortage each driver was issued with a manual which set out tyre maintenance standards and a training programme was instituted to acquaint drivers with the standards and methods prescribed. The Military Police on duty on the main gate were given a Schrader master gauge with instructions to test the tyres of every unit vehicle each day. Drivers were not allowed to leave the area until they had the correct air pressure in all tyres. On 7 December 1944 there was a 'Tires for Victory Contest' when winners of the best written articles were given passes and furloughs as prizes.

It was also necessary for the hospital to consider the economy of fuel used for the fires and boilers. The following measures to conserve energy were decided upon:

"1. Mixing all the fine coal and coke so as to burn all fuel that could be burned.
2. Closing all wards and ward tents that had less then 50 percentage of beds occupied by patients.

Old Glory flying at the 155th. (155th General Hospital Archives)

Flagpole with flag flying at half mast, possibly for the death of President Roosevelt in April 1945. Photo shows walkway around it and Admin building in the background. (Walter Lochbaum)

3. *Returning all ashes in order to use any unburned coal or coke.*
4. *Raking up of all coal and coke storage piles in order to prevent excess loss of coal and coke on the ground.*
5. *Checking of temperatures in wards to prevent excessive firing of stoves."*
(155th General Hospital Archives)

Covered walkway. (Walter Lochbaum)

View of Malvern Hills from Admin building. (Walter Lochbaum)

Motor Pool. (155th General Hospital Archives)

Like the 93rd the Mess Department of the 155th had to cut out wastage through plate checks at the end of a meal. The Department operated three mess halls, one for the officers, one for enlisted men and one for patients. The Patients' Mess was composed of two units, the main kitchen where regular diets were prepared and the diet kitchen in which soft liquid and special diets were made up. Ambulatory patients walked to the mess hall for their food while approximately twenty food carts were loaded to transport food to the wards of those who were bed bound. Originally both carts and patients used the same doorway but the diet kitchen was soon established as a separate room with a separate entrance constructed in the outside wall to prevent congestion caused when carts were exiting through the same doorway that the ambulatory patients were queuing.

View of the 155th hospital with motor pool. (155th General Hospital Archives)

Motor Pool in the snow.
(Walter Lochbaum)

Nurse collecting coal and coke to use in stoves.
(Battleship Cove Museum)

When the155th assumed operations on Site Two in July it had 999 patients, the bed capacity being 1082, expandable to 1367. As the number of casualties arriving at the hospital increased it was necessary to place convalescent patients in double decked beds in wards and use 17 overflow winterised ward tents. One tent, named the 'plaster tent' was used for applying plaster casts and manipulations under general anaesthetic.

In October 1944 the hospital was designated a Thoracic Center, this caused a considerate influx of patients from hospitals within the 12th Hospital Center and an increase in the number of operations carried out. On 1st November the Thoracic section was moved into a group of buildings originally designed as a venereal disease section but at this point being used by the Convalescent Training Section. With the increase in patient load during the early months of 1945 an additional officer was assigned to the Thoracic Section in February.

Nurses collecting coal for use in billets. (Battleship Cove Museum)

Patients mess. (155th General Hospital Archives)

Ward tents erected on the ends of wards. (155th General Hospital Archives)

Front of the Thoracic Center. (155th General Hospital Archives)

Many of the cases referred to the Thoracic section required the removal of foreign objects. Before this could be done it was necessary for Doctors to decide whether the object should be removed or not. In some cases it was less dangerous to leave the object where it was. The doctors made the decision by looking at the size of the object and the amount of pain it was causing. Objects less than 1cm in diameter were removed only if they were jagged or irregular or if they were located close to some vital structure. In some cases if the foreign body were in or near to the heart or in the upper abdomen or the liver it was decided that it was better to return patients to the U.S. to be operated on.

Bob Elgin was a Surgeon's Assistant and Scrub Nurse. He remembers assisting with heart and lung surgery. The doctors had to operate without the aid of heart and lung machines. Ether, which could cause post operative problems, was used as a general anaesthetic. Gloves had to be reused and needles resharpened after surgery. The only chemical used to stop infection was sulphur. The section carried out other kinds of surgery too. Bob remembers that the surgeon, Major Mainzer, would always whistle 'Mighty like a Rose' while operating on haemorrhoids.

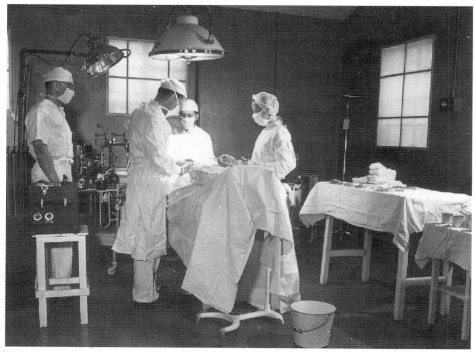

155th General Hospital Operating Theatre. (155th General Hospital Archives)

There were two main operating rooms, each with two operating tables and one smaller room with one table used for infected cases. There was another large room which was used to sterilise tools and also for coffee breaks. Bob shared a hut with the man who drove the supply trucks for the unit. He got him the ingredients

Bob Elgin in whites ready for surgery and in dress uniform. (Bob Elgin)

for baking bread which he gave to one of the female civilian workers on the base. She would bake four loaves of bread, keeping one for herself and the other three were eaten by Bob and his colleagues with their coffee.

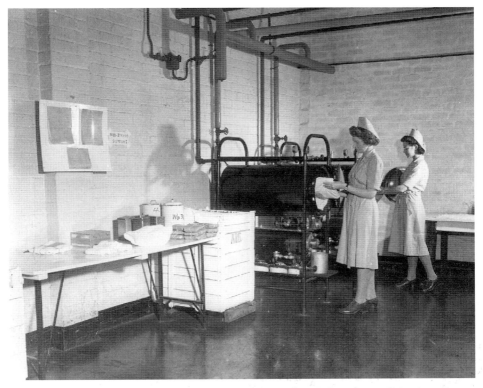

Nurses with autoclave for sterilising instruments. (155th General Hospital Archives)

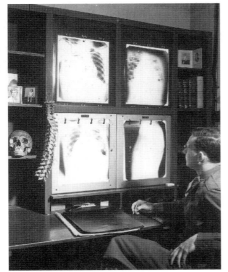

The X-ray service worked closely with the thoracic surgeon section. Examinations were usually made to determine the location of foreign bodies and/or collections of fluid. The enlisted technicians in the department devised certain innovations which were incorporated into the services offered by the department.

X-ray Section of the 155th. (155th General Hospital Archives)

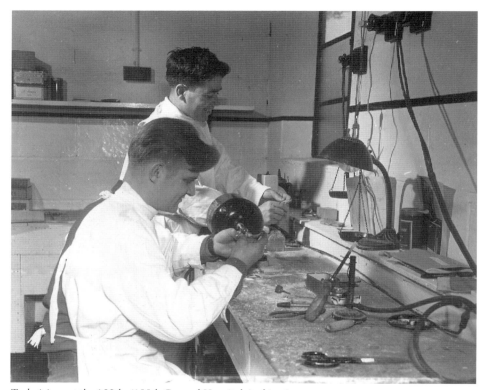

Technicians at the 155th. (155th General Hospital Archives)

Several items were constructed for the use of the department such as a light arc welder, a chassis to transport a portable X-ray machine and a film fact board- designed to keep the technicians constantly informed of the changes and film factors which were being used at all times. The X-ray Department also found it necessary to devise a procedure for using convalescent patients to transport the non- ambulatory orthopaedic patients to and from the X-ray department so that ward personnel could continue with their other duties.

Another busy section of the hospital was the orthopaedic surgical section. The majority of fracture cases admitted to the hospital had incurred injury anything from four to thirty days prior to admission to the hospital. By this point a plaster cast had been applied in most cases but it was often necessary to remove the plaster, place the part in skeletal traction and then reapply plaster to include the joint above and below the fracture.

A large number of these patients were paratroopers. Norm Johnson remembers being on an orthopaedic ward:

> *"Full of paratroopers with body casts and legs hanging in the air in trapezes."*

Orthopaedic Patients at the 155th. (Battleship Cove Museum)

Norm and some of his fellow patients would often attempt to walk down the road from the hospital to the local pub. He recalls that one of the paratrooper patients had a cast on his leg and was on crutches. After a few beers he forgot about his crutches and walked back to the hospital. By the time he reached the ward his cast was in shreds. After the doctor had replaced the cast several times the patient's clothes were taken away but even this did not stop him as he continued to walk down to the pub in his pyjamas and dressing gown.

Sometimes Norm and another paratrooper friend would 'borrow' bikes to ride around the hospital and the neighbouring hospitals to see if they could find anyone from their unit. This activity had to stop when they were warned that one of the majors from the hospital was looking for his 'borrowed' bike.

Norm also remembers the night when one of the paratroopers woke up yelling from a nightmare and tried to climb out of the window. He and a few of the other patients had to grab him and hold onto him until an orderly came. Norm also remembers hearing a big explosion one night which everyone thought was a buzz bomb. He recalls:

> *"Those of us, who could walk, crawl or navigate left the ward for the woods."*

The next morning they found out that there was a British practice range nearby and realised that the noise they had heard was British armament.

Physiotherapy for orthopaedic patients was instituted as early as ten days after injury as experience proved that better results obtained if treatment was begun at an early date. Apparatus was devised to exercise limbs in traction. The staff in the orthopaedic section made equipment when necessary. They acquired equipment for making orthopaedic shoe corrections and also improvised a special glove for patients

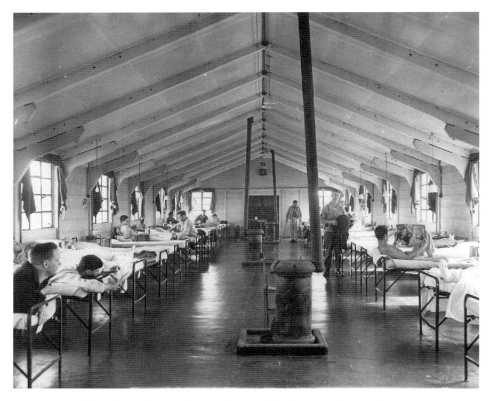

Patients in Wards at the 155th. (155th General Hospital Archives) and (Battleship Cove Museum)

with nerve palsies of the hand. This glove was attached to the arm above the elbow by elastic cords and fashioned to replace the paralysed muscles and tendons and hold the extremities in normal position.

The hospital also had two wards for the use of the Neuropsychiatric Section. It was necessary for some psychiatric

patients to be treated on other wards because of their other injuries. Emphasis was placed on individual psychotherapy rather than group treatment:

> *"This procedure purposed to give to the patient adequate insight into his condition with a knowledge of the underlying mechanism involved ... Armed with these new acquisitions he departed from the psychiatric ward much better prepared to face the problems of war."* (155th General Hospital Archives)

In spring the section encouraged recreational activities outside like gardening. A programme of physical conditioning and military orientation was instituted. The section aimed to minimise the emotional trauma of transition from patient to soldier status by carrying out recreational and military activities side by side supervised by a uniformed officer.

The 155th also maintained a shock, emergency fracture and burn team supervised by medical officers. This team functioned in the case of emergency, day or night, to deal with incoming casualties. It also dealt with civilian emergencies. There were several times when the team was called out to incidents in the local area.

A number of American vehicles from the hospitals were involved in motor accidents. This was sometimes because the drivers were accustomed to driving on the other side of the road. Dr. David Parker remembers several accidents involving American trucks and British bicycles. He remembers one incident when a cyclist got hit by an American truck and broke his pelvis. He was taken to a British hospital but because they didn't have a urologist Dr. Parker was asked to operate. He remembers that the nurses didn't realise he was American until he took off his operating gown and put his uniform on to return to base. They didn't notice his accent because he was talking through a mask.

In February 1944 a black American truck driver, Private William J. Brookes was discovered dead close to his truck which was found overturned at the bottom of an embankment above British Camp Hill Road. It was thought that Brookes had jumped out of the truck as it went over the embankment. Stewart Trigg, a local lad, remembers seeing the truck which had gone right through the wall at the top of the very steep slope on the Malvern side of British Camp. In May of that year two soldiers were killed and two seriously injured when their jeep overturned at a bend in the road by the church at Guarlford.

The emergency teams from the hospitals at Blackmore Park were also called out to several plane crashes in the area. In April 1944 a Beaufighter crashed in South Wood. One man managed to get out of the plane but he had broken his shoulder and couldn't help the Australian pilot. When Charles Williams, a 20 year old farm worker arrived on the scene he was able to pull the pilot, along with his seat, out of the burning plane. Just as Charles had dragged the man to a nearby ditch about 12 yards away the plane exploded.

American ambulances arrived at the scene but would not go near the plane until the ammunition stopped exploding. Eventually they were able to take the pilot to Blackmore Park where they treated him for burns and a broken pelvis. At first they thought he was dying, as he was bleeding from the mouth, but later they found that this was due to the fact that his false teeth had gone down his throat. After a fortnight he regained consciousness and made a good recovery. Later Charles Williams received the British Empire Medal for his actions.

In June a Beaufort from Defford, a local R.A.F. airfield where top secret work on radar was carried out, was seen to be having difficulties in the Malvern area.

Spitfire that ran off the end of the runway at Pershore Airfield. (Paul Simmons)

The pilot bailed out and landed safely near a farm, while the plane hit the ground and exploded some yards away from the farm buildings. Within minutes ambulances from Blackmore Park were on the scene. An ambulance took the pilot to Merebrook Hospital for a check up but he had escaped lightly and was flying again the next day.

The crew of a Canadian bomber that crashed near the 155th hospital area were not so lucky. The men of the 155th searched but they couldn't find any survivors. Paul Simmons remembers coming across some parachute ropes with a torso attached to them and also he picked up a glove with a hand in it but the British authorities gave instructions for everything to be left in situ.

Malvern News 27/5/1944.

RESCUED PILOT FROM BLAZING PLANE

Guarlford Farm Worker's Gallant Act

When an aircraft crashed on April 22 at Guarlford, Malvern, and burst into flames a young farm worker, Charles Richard Williams, of Archer's Cottage, Sherrard's Green, forced his way through the flames, pulled out the pilot, who was severely injured and unconscious and carried him clear of the wreckage.

Williams who is 20 years of age and stands over six feet in height, is employed by Mr. Ronald H. Smith, of Guarlford Court. He told a reporter: "I was working in a rickyard when I saw the plane overhead, apparently in difficulties. I saw it dive down and heard a crash, and then saw a cloud of smoke. I raced as fast as I could across the fields for a quarter-of-a-mile and saw a R.A.F. sergeant, who had a broken collar bone, near the plane.

"I asked if there was anybody in the plane and he said, 'Yes, the pilot.' I ran to the blazing wreckage, crawled underneath and dragged out the pilot, still attached to the seat.

"It was very hot, as the whole of the machine was on fire and as I left the plane ammunition began to explode. The pilot's face was covered in blood, and I could see he was badly injured. I dragged him clear of the wreckage, and while I went for the ambulance my father Mr. T. Williams and Mr. G. H. Wall, of Grove House Farm, carried him to a ditch."

Except for a few cuts and bruises Williams was uninjured.

Chapter 8
155th General Hospital – Convalescent Section

With the large number of patients arriving at the 155th a system was put into place so that patients could be transported to the wards quickly and smoothly. The officers in charge of Receiving and Evacuation and two other medical officers boarded the hospital train about 30 minutes before arrival at Malvern Link Station. Each patient was tagged with a coloured tag bearing the number of the ward to which he was to be admitted. Four colours were used to correspond to four dispersal points in the hospital area, from where the patients were taken to their wards. The patients' baggage was often picked up from the station later.

155th General Hospital administration building personnel. L-R: Sgt John Edmondson, Tec. 5 Sgt Aranson, S/Sgt Max Valoris and Tec. 5 Richard Statler.

The hospital also took patients that had been airlifted in from the continent. Two ward tents were set up at Pershore Airfield and two enlisted technicians were placed on temporary duty there. Paul Simmons was based at the airfield from March to May 1945 where he lived in one of the ward tents. He and the other technician would change dressings, give transfusions and transfer the wounded to ambulances which would take them to the hospital best suited to deal with their condition.

Staff Sergeant Walter Lochbaum, who worked in the Quartermasters Section of the unit, was responsible for supervising the personnel who handled and stored the patients' possessions. He and his men would make two trips a day to collect the baggage from the stations in Great Malvern. At one of the stations the station master and his wife would usually have ready a cup of tea and homemade biscuits for the men.

Sgt Bill Lochbaum, Private Eric Sehl and ? in Quartermaster Stores at 155th. (Walter Lochbaum)

Walter remembers one occasion, while doing a luggage pick up at the railway station, that all the traffic was stopped for the Royal vehicle carrying the King, Queen and their two daughters from Balmoral Castle to Buckingham Palace. Walter remembers clearly seeing the Princesses Elizabeth and Margaret sitting in their window seats while the Malvern people lined the streets waving their flags.

Walter would take the bags back to the hospital to be listed on an inventory:

"When the luggage was inventoried, an itemised count of each item was listed and the patient received a copy of their evaluation. The paratroop patients were most concerned about their boots. Some even had us bring their boots to the hospital ward where they would securely tie them to

the bed posts for safe keeping. When the patient returned to active duty, a complete new outfit was issued. If they returned to a ship for return to the States the clothing count was made and additional clothing was issued to the patient."

Most of the patients wounded in battle were transferred, after their wounds had healed, to the Convalescent Training Section, where they were given a trial period of reconditioning including supervised marches, athletics and other physical training.

The Convalescent Training Section was run as a detachment of the hospital and consisted of patients whose treatment was completed and were awaiting evacuation to duty or to a convalescent hospital. Some patients awaiting return to the U.S. were also transferred to this section. The section was commanded by an attached infantry officer who was assisted by two other officer convalescent patients. Convalescent non-commissioned officers acted as First Sergeant and Platoon Sergeant. Convalescent training patients were issued fatigues to distinguish them from other patients.

When the Thoracic Section moved into the convalescent building in November 1944 the men constructed two temporary buildings from salvaged lumber with wooden walls and floor and a canvas covered roof. One of the buildings was for use as a gymnasium and one as a dayroom.

On admission to the Convalescent Section patients were awarded a grade, A or B. Most patients were given Grade B on admission. The training for these patients consisted of light callisthenics and progressive hikes of from one to seven miles. As the trainees condition improved they were advanced to Grade A. In this group the training consisted of daily hikes of from one to four miles and a weekly hike of eleven miles as well as more strenuous callisthenics.

Classes were held daily in the gymnasium under the supervision of a technical sergeant who had specialist training in recondition work. Special attention was given to stiff hands, arms, shoulders, legs, back and feet. Each trainee was examined weekly by medical offices to evaluate progress. The patient's capacity for work was judged by the staff in this section who had to decide whether the patients were genuinely unwell or merely attempting to avoid going back into a combat situation:

"Gastric-intestinal patients that were X-ray negative, dubious asthmatics and 'unwilling' soldiers were kept busy by a trial of progressive exercise." (155th General Hospital Archives)

Whenever possible patients were returned to replacement depots where decisions were made as to whether patients were returned to full or limited assignment. By January the convalescent training section was living away from the main hospital in tents to:

"...emphasize the break away from hospital life and to begin the toughening up process for duty." (155th General Hospital Archives)

On 6th February 1945 the highest patient census was reached with a total of 1702 patients. This was partly because this hospital, along with four others in the Malvern area, was established as a Z.I. Center i.e. Patients to be returned to the U.S. from other hospitals were sent to the Malvern hospitals while awaiting passage. At the same time the hospital was receiving frequent convoys of patients for general treatment and convalescence and special cases of thoracic surgery.

In February changes were made to the convalescent training programme and the section was divided into groups who trained separately. The officer group trained under the command of the ranking patient officer. The trench foot group had exercise that depended on the severity of their condition. Part of this group could manage a moderate amount of walking. After a weekly four to six mile hike feet were examined by a medical officer. When the condition of the feet warranted it the patient could be transferred into the B (limited exercise) group. The remaining part of the Trench foot group was prevented from walking because of the state of their feet. This group remained indoors most of the time and took general callisthenics and hand to hand combat practice. Special attention was given to foot straightening exercises.

The other group that exercised separately were those awaiting shipment to the U.S. They had supervised exercises from the ward master and in some cases the ranking non commissioned officer patient. This was necessary:

"...since the segregation of patients to be returned to the zone of the interior is almost imperative in order to prevent their influence upon patients who will return to duty Z.I. Fever is thus eliminated." (155th General Hospital Archives)

Michael Samberg was one of the Z.I. patients transferred to the 155th. He had received minor shot gun wounds while serving as a rifle man with the 26th Infantry Division in January 1945. Michael recalls:

"When examined it was determined that my feet had suffered moderately severe frost damage with impending gangrene. I had been unaware of the damage since my feet were numb. The pain came later."

Michael was put on the Queen Mary in mid February to sail for the U.S. He was discharged from military service for disability from a convalescent hospital in August 1945.

Paul Simmons remembers meeting another Z.I. patient at the 155th who was a neighbour of his from back home. Apparently he had been wounded while

Paul Simmons outside Enlisted Man's Quarters at Blackmore Park. (Paul Simmons)

Paul Simmons outside Enlisted Man's Quarters at Blackmore Park. (Paul Simmons)

serving with General Patton and was now awaiting shipment home:

> "He borrowed five pounds from me and then shipped out without paying me back. I saw him after we were home and I asked him about the money. He said he gave it to one of the orderlies to give back to me because he got shipped out too quick to see me personally."

Paul decided that he should take this as a lesson in life – never to lend money to a friend.

From February 12 1945, when the hospital was full to capacity it underwent reorganisation and the staffing quota was reduced. Surplus officers and enlisted personnel were transferred to duty with other hospitals. Two nurses and two enlisted men were placed on temporary duty with hospital ships evacuating patients to the Zone of the Interior. Medical officers, Nurses and enlisted technicians were placed on temporary duty from time to time accompanying patients to ports of embarkation.

Four nurses and 30 enlisted men from the 155th were designated by other hospitals as needing to return to the U.S. for further observation, treatment and disposition. Of the 30 men, 20 were former combat soldiers assigned to the medical department of the 155th and found to be physically or psychologically unfit for further duty after a trial period.

Bob Elgin recalls:

> "When the Battle of the Bulge was in full force we got wounded in large numbers. Needing men to replace the men at the front we began sending some of our men and keeping the wounded who were able to replace the men sent to the front. This scattered our original personnel in all directions."

Personnel who were transferred out were partly replaced with limited assignment personnel i.e. men who had gone through the hospital system who had been declared physically unfit for further duty with combat organisations but not badly wounded enough to be sent home.

Bob Elgin remembers a young Irish lad called Nathan Calhoun, who joined the hospital and was billeted in Bob's hut:

> *"Nathan came to me one day with a letter he had received form his parents in Ireland. They had only one cow that had become deathly sick. With the war there were no veterinarians or any drugs to treat the cow. I was able to get the needed drugs and other materials he needed. I had a friend who piloted B17s out of a field near Birmingham. From the same field the RAF had smaller fighter planes. These planes were shuttled over to a field in Ireland. We were able to get Nathan a three day pass (the pass was only good in England). It took a lot of work to get him into the small plane but we did get him to Ireland and back in three days and we did save the cow."*

From 1 May 1945 a point system was introduced for American forces serving overseas. Personnel with the required number of points were sent home to the U.S. Officer replacements for the personnel leaving were drawn from other hospital units that had closed down and thirty six enlisted men were sent from the 12th Reinforcement Depot to replace enlisted personnel.

Shortly after the V.E. Day hospital trains ceased to arrive and on May 21 the 12th Hospital Centre received orders reducing the official bed capacity. This involved taking down the ward tents and returning them to the Quartermaster. Supplies of beds, mattresses, bed linen and bed side tables were returned to the suppliers.

Orders requested that surplus British mattresses be used instead of American mattresses in the wards so that American mattresses could be retuned. Orders recommended that P.O.W. labour should be used to take down electrical equipment and lumber from the tents.

Despite the sharp falling off of casualties during the period around V.E. Day. Admissions to the Thoracic section did not decrease until the latter part of May and surgical activity continued into June. The hospital had orders to shut on 8 June and all patients were evacuated by 16 June. The 155th was directed to prepare for overseas movement.

Once the hospital was closed the unit was directed to prepare for redeployment an intensive training programme consisting of lectures, training films on malaria, mosquito control, skin diseases, skin hygiene, intestinal disease and geography and climate of the Pacific was instituted.

In preparation for redeployment packing cases were constructed and stencilling of equipment and baggage was carried out. All steam and electrical equipment was dismantled and disconnected for return to depots.

Formal retreat at 155th General Hospital, Blackmore Park. (Battleship Cove Museum)

Retreat at Blackmore Park. (155th General Hospital Archives)

Photos of Retreat at Blackmore Park. (155th General Hospital Archives)

The organisation departed from Malvern Wells on 11 July 1945 by rail to the Port of Embarkation in Glasgow. On 12 July they sailed on the Aquitania and arrived in New York on 19th July. At Camp Shanks, New York the personnel were given 30 days furlough and leaves. On 14 September three quarters of the personnel assembled at Camp Sibert, Alabama to commence a training programme including road marches, organised athletics, orientation and instruction in arctic and tropical sanitation. The personnel were also taught carbine familiarisation, rifle, marksmanship and classes in the use of grenades, mines and booby traps. Fortunately, due to the end of the war in the Pacific, the 155th General Hospital was inactivated on 21 September 1945.

Chapter 9
155th General Hospital – Special Service Section and Red Cross Unit

Each group of personnel at the 155th had their own building to relax in when off duty. An officer's club was set up in a building which had originally been intended as an Officers' Mess in the Officers' Quarters area, while the nurses formed a club that was located, in their living area. The N.C.O.s organised a non coms club and decorated a Nissen hut for their use and two buildings were redecorated and refurnished in the detachment area for the enlisted men.

P.X. for use of patients and detachment men in their free time. (155th General Hospital Archives)

Barber's Shop at the 155th. (155th General Hospital Archives)

As with the 93rd the Special Service Section and Red Cross units worked closely together to cater for the educational and recreational needs of the personnel at the hospital. Weekly bus trips to places of historic interest in nearby cities and villages were conducted for ambulatory patients and detachment personnel. Unfortunately, because of the need for tyre conservation, the trips became less frequent from December 1944.

Both the Red Cross and Special Service organised sporting tournaments. An interdepartmental softball league was set up which provided athletic competitions among the departments and sections at the hospital. The medical department softball team played several games against teams from nearby hospitals and a softball team comprised of Royal Canadian Air Force personnel. On Sundays, weather permitting, the Red Cross girls took patients out to watch nearby football games. Patients with casts were not given passes. Colonel Gantt was particularly anxious that they should have the opportunity to go off base so the girls:-

> *"...filled the trucks with canes and crutches and took turns going out with them."* (155th General Hospital Red Cross Archives)

The Special Service set up an Information and Education Programme Office in 1945 and enlisted men were required to attend one hour of discussion and lectures each week. Enlisted men's discussions were held in the 'war talk tent' which contained blackboards charts and maps. Discussions centred on such topics as International Relations, Post War Problems and Planning. From time to time lecturers sponsored by the British Ministry of Information discussed topics of international interest with the men.

The British Ministry of Information were also responsible for inviting patients to events in the locality such as tea dances, garden parties and theatre parties. As Madeline Talbott, the Senior Recreation Worker with the Red Cross unit wrote:

"...these have highlighted the month of February and March (1945) and turned our grey pajamed patients into social butterflies ... You should see them when they turn up at the appointed hour ... faces and shoes shining like mirrors and uniforms creased to super sharpness." (155th General Hospital Red Cross Archives)

The Red Cross unit for the 155th was comprised of 5 workers who arrived at Blackmore Park on 16th July 1944 when they worked alongside the 90th General Hospital Red Cross unit for a week. On July 24 the 155th assumed all responsibilities for Red Cross duties in the hospital.

On arrival the girls found that Red Cross facilities were dotted around the hospital so they put in a request to have the complete use of one of the buildings, which Colonel Gantt agreed to. The building had several rooms. The first large room housed the library with writing desks, phonograph, radiogram and piano; the second large room housed the snooker table, two ping pong tables and a small pool table. The two small rooms were used for supplies and an office, and a medium sized room, which became known as the 'Doodle room' was used as a craft shop. Moving all the Red Cross activities into one building meant that it was easier to supervise activities and more workers could be released to work on the wards with non ambulatory patients.

The library had a large selection of books but the majority were out of date and of little interest to the men. Irma Ekstrom, the Staff Aide, sorted out the newer editions (post 1932) and put them into one section. Each month Special Service passed on new paperbacks to the girls for the library. Irma reported that:

"The paperbound books have popular appeal because they are comparatively new books, they are easy to handle and are colourful and attractive." (155th General Hospital American Red Cross Archives) Around thirty to forty books were left on each ward and changed regularly for patients to read.

For the first few weeks at Blackmore Park Colonel Gantt requested that the girls concentrate on working on the wards making bed patients their priority-supplying movies, shows and crafts. With this in mind the girls made arrangements for the Special Service to show films on wards four days and three evenings a week.

The girls began to implement a craft programme but on arrival there was a shortage of craft materials. For the first few weeks ambulatory patients did crafts alongside the bed patients in the wards which made things difficult as it meant each ward needed tools, materials and supervision from the girls. Crafts included making leather wallets, picture frames, watch bands, wool and cotton mat weaving, string belts, string cigarette cases, clay modelling, plexi glass rings and scrap books.

Armed Services Editions of paperback books distributed to forces personnel. (Author's collection)

The girls also received several requests from medical officers for plasticine for some of the patients to use to give them practice in manipulating their fingers while giving them something constructive to do. Madeline Talbott reported about the soft toy making:

"Some strange breeds of felt animals were designed by the patients to send home to their youngsters. They really enjoyed making them even though they took a bit of kidding from some of the bachelors." (155th General Hospital Red Cross Archives)

Later model aeroplanes were added to the list of crafts and model plane contests were held. Just before Christmas the patients made items for the Christmas Fair organised by the W.V.S. that the 93rd had contributed to.

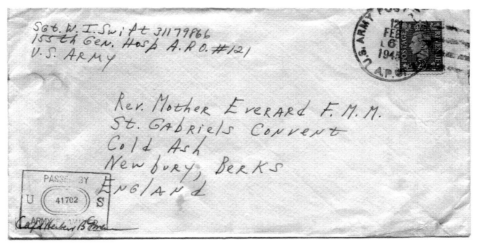

Letter sent from a Sergeant with the 155th. (Author's collection)

The girls decided to divide the wards into four groups so that each worker could supervise a group of eight wards, apart from the secretary. The girls aimed to visit each ward at least three times a week. The Chief Nurse ensured that at least two nurses came to help the Red Cross each evening so that the girls could cover more wards. It was important for the girls to contact each patient to determine his needs, whether it be comfort articles or someone to write a letter for him. As new patients arrived the Red Cross attempted to see them all as soon as possible. When a large group of ambulatory patients arrived hot chocolate and cookies were served and cigarettes and gum distributed. The following week each patient was contacted and given the necessary comfort articles. Many of the patients had lost all their possessions en route and needed ditty bags. Like the 93rd the girls found that their stocks were soon depleted.

In October 1944 the 12th Medical Center requested that the Red Cross girls should go to the train station to see off the patients travelling back to the U.S. By this point stocks were so low that all the girls could distribute were gum and candy. Cigarettes were the item most requested but because of the shortages the girls only gave them out to patients who arrived with no funds to buy their own.

On their first Sunday at the 155th the girls held 'Open House' in the Red Cross building. Over 150 patients enjoyed hot chocolate and cookies, played the piano, sang, played checkers and chatted. Some of the senior officers like Colonel Gantt, Chief Nurse Major Aycock and Executive Officer Major Pickering dropped in. It was such a success that the girls decided to repeat the idea every Sunday. At the end of 1944 the girls reported that between Open House parties and birthday cakes, which the girls made for the patients with cookies and chocolate sauce, about 100lb of Hershey's chocolate had been used each month.

At the end of the first week Madeline Talbott reported:

> *Our first week 'in the harness' was a whirlwind. We carried on the crafts in the wards, picked up the old books, magazines and games and distributed new ones. The supply room was kept open every morning so that ambulatory patients could get the craft materials to take to the other wards. We had movies in the Theatre Tuesday, Thursday and Saturday nights and a matinee on Sunday. On July 28 thirty patients went by special bus to Worcester to attend the Vaudeville show at the Royal Theatre.*" (155th General Hospital Red Cross Archives)

The Red Cross Clubmobile, based in Malvern, was a regular visitor to the 155th. On Wednesday nights the girls from the clubmobile distributed coffee and doughnuts to the patients. Food carts were borrowed from the Mess Hall so that urns of coffee and baskets of doughnuts could be taken around the wards. Ambulatory patients pushed the food cart and assisted with the distribution of coffee while the clubmobile girls passed out the doughnuts with the help of one of the Red Cross Staff. In this way the entire hospital was covered in one and a half hours.

In July 1944 a 'Doughnut Dugout' was opened in Malvern. Doughnuts and coffee could be bought there. In August a Red Cross Club was also opened in the town. Each hospital in the Malvern area was entered into a competition to decorate a room representing the hospital and also to furnish refreshments for approximately 150 people. One of the detachment men drew a sketch on the wall in the 155th's room to remain as a permanent fixture while the girls dressed the rest of the room in autumn

American Red Cross Club Malvern. (53rd General Hospital Archives)

The same building today being used by an Estate Agent. (M.Collins)

leaf shapes. The 155th didn't win the competition but Lilian Thiessen, the Junior Recreation worker felt that:

> "Our efforts were not in vain as the results were most attractive but the room drawn to be decorated was too small to show off its beauty." (155th General Hospital Red Cross Archives)

A number of the detachment personnel were willing to give their spare time to help the Red Cross to entertain the patients. Several were talented pianists and played classical, swing and Spanish piano music on the wards. One of the men sang solos on the wards, giving a good impersonation of the Inkspots while another sketched pin up girls and made greetings cards for the patients.

Two of the detachment men were assigned to the Red Cross unit. One took responsibility for the movie projector and cleaning the Theatre while the other acted as a general handyman. As the hospital had only one projector at the beginning it had a heavy

Malvern news 7/10/1944.

RED CROSS CLUB OPENS

Americans Design Rooms

Malvern's first American Red Cross Club opened informally on Friday, when a number of local residents, including Councillor T. Cook, Colonel Wheeler, Miss Day (W.V.S.), Miss Morgan (C.A.B.), Mrs. March, Mrs. A. Harrison and Mr. A. W. Priestley, inspected the rooms, which had been decorated by American soldiers, each room having been taken over by U.S. hospitals in the 12th U.S. Medical Centre. Great interest was evoked by the original colour schemes and their execution. After voting had taken place, Miss Blum (the Director) announced the result.

The winning room, a long-shaped rather dark room, had been transformed into an art gallery, with a frieze representing the U.S. man at war in every service, with some of his "pin-up girls." Gay and bold brushwork was allied to a good imagination, so that the result was entirely amusing and delightful. The winners received a vase and the runners-up a book on Worcestershire history. The runners-up had designed their room in a patriotic mood, with flags of the Allies well in evidence.

Another room was gay with autumn leaves and streamers, another had mural designs illustrating the lighter side of rehabilitation.

In this latter room a monster cake was on view, made at one of the hospitals and wishing the club every success. The main decoration was the flag of the U.S. in marzipan.

The judges were entertained to doughnuts and tea, and were cordially thanked by Miss Blum. Two American colonels also attended, and expressed their pleasure at what was being done for the welfare of U.S. personnel.

A meeting was then held at which plans were made for the setting up and staffing of an information centre. There were many offers of help, but anyone wishing to give a few hours every week, or even more time, are asked to get in touch with Miss Blum, or with Colonel Wheeler.

In the evening a dance took place, which was enjoyed by a large crowd. Local girls acted as hostesses.

workload. Movies were shown four days a week in the Theatre then two days and one afternoon in the wards. The seventh day was spent cleaning and oiling the machine. In September Madeline Talbott reported that:

> *Our one prayer is that the movie projector will not give out."* (155th General Hospital Red Cross Archives).

In November the Special Service obtained another projector so the workload was reduced for the Red Cross projector. Madeline was relieved as she stated in her November report:

> *"The machine has held up very well due to the interest and special care given to it by Pvt. Gorder, the detachment man who is one of the men assigned to the R.C. However many of the lamps are getting scarce and it is hoped that the supply recently ordered will be available as will the bulbs."* (155th General Hospital Red Cross Archives)

The two enlisted men, Private Chris Gorder and Private Frantz also decorated the Theatre. Madeline describes the results of the decorating as:

> *"It was transformed from a cold, bare building into a warm, cheerful and inviting theatre. The walls were painted cream and brown, the glaring overhead lights were covered with shades which have coloured stars shining through."* (155th General Hospital Red Cross Archives)

Private Chris Gorder. Detachment man assigned to the Red Cross. (Paul Simmons)

During 1944 the Red Cross installed a public address system in the hospital. The control panel was located in the Red Cross building and speakers placed in each of the 39 wards as well as various other buildings on the post. Once installed the system was kept in daily operation from 10 o'clock in the morning to half past nine in the evening. When the phonograph did arrive it was in constant use, even when not being used for the P.A. system and the Red Cross complained about the:

"…high mortality rate on records due to use first and carelessness second." (155th General Hospital Red Cross Archives)

The P.A. system was also used for daily announcements. Patients and detachment men presented some programmes for the entertainment of the entire hospital and at other times radio programmes were transmitted. For two weeks one of the patients who had formally been a radio announcer took over the duties of Master of Ceremonies. One successful use of the P.A. system was the G.I. Joe Quiz contest broadcast to the wards on Sunday nights. Each ward was visited before the quiz and given explanations and one mimeographed form for the answer sheet. The winning ward received the prize of a 'party' consisting of ice cream, cake etc.

In October the Red Cross put on a Halloween party. Jack O Lanterns were made out of corrugated boxes painted orange with faces out of them. Bat and witch silhouettes were stuck on the walls and large black cats sat over the doors. The party was so popular that some had to sit on tables and on window sills. The girls had planned for 75 patients as they knew that there were dances arranged in the locality. As the patients came through the door the girls gave them a number but at 175 they ran out of numbers. One of the patients came dressed in a sheet. Lots of games like apple bobbing, darts and relay races were played:

"Another contest was eating string to get a delicious dried apricot. An apricot was tied in the middle of the string. A patient took either end of the string in his mouth and they had to eat the string to get to the apricot. Its not so easy. The big game of the night was the old water feeding one. We had eight tables and two patients sitting opposite each other at each one. They were blindfolded and given a bottle filled with water and a spoon. They had to pour water onto the spoon and feed the person opposite. The floor was well cleaned that night we might add. … We used the snooker table for a blowing contest. Sides of six were chosen and lined up on either side of the table, six ping pong balls were placed down on the centre. When the signal was given they started to blow, each side trying to get all the balls in the pockets on the opposite side. We ended the party with hot chocolate and our favourite chocolate covered cookie cake." (155th General Hospital Red Cross Archives)

In November preparations were begun for Christmas. Each ward was supplied with a small tree courtesy of the Army Mess Fund, coloured paper, Christmas templates and powder paints. Madeline Talbott found that:

> *"Each ward was outstanding in its originally. There were nativity scenes, Santa Claus in jeeps, reindeers, fireplaces with G.I. socks hung on the mantle, bells and holly. The Christmas trees were decorated with bits of this and that- icicles from tin cans, fruit life savers, tin foil, popcorn, red berries, cotton paper flowers and little dolls made of matches. With the powdered paints they painted the windows. Such artistic talent we never dreamed of – there were of course all the lovely Christmas scenes with snow, Santa Claus and his reindeer, snowmen of all kinds, even a little sign pointing to the United States saying '3000 miles'. We didn't believe they could do so much with so little. The nurses and wardmen entered into the spirit and worked as hard on the decorations as the patients did."* (155th General Hospital Red Cross Archives)

The patients also used the powder paints to paint on the Recreation Hall windows. One of the enlisted men made special shades for the lights in the lounge and theatre. He also made a fireplace with lighted logs and G.I. stockings hanging from it, holly covered the top and two candles which were lit every evening. Over the big double door leading into the Games Room was a large 'Sad Sack' Christmas scene drawn by one of the patients. There was a tree decorated with tin ornaments, painted ping pong balls, gold and silver angels, cellophane icicles and lights sent from the U.S. by a former officer patient.

Chapel at 155th General Hospital decorated for Christmas. (155th General Hospital Archives)

On the Saturday before Christmas eighteen choir boys from one of the nearby churches came to the hospital to sing. They broadcast Christmas carols through the P.A. system to the whole hospital at meal time. At 7.30 they put on a Christmas service in the chapel and afterwards had supper in the Doodle Room. They left with a Christmas package of candy and gum.

On Christmas Eve the girls started early to complete last minute jobs like trimming the four Santa suits, made of dyed red bed sheets, with 'ermine'. At 6.00 in the evening the girls held 'Open House'. Hundreds of sandwiches had been made which disappeared almost instantly with the help of the cider. A special patient talent show was put on in the Games Room and broadcast over the P.A. system. Just before it went off air:

> *"…our four Santa clauses roared in complete even to sleigh bells, sang a song and dashed out to start their rounds. The four detachment men who were Santa Claus will probably never know how much their nonsense meant to the patients. In each ward they picked up the barracks bags filled with the Christmas boxes which had been sent for the patients and gave each boy his present with a loud and gay 'Merry Christmas'."* (155th General Hospital Red Cross Archives)

The favourite article in the Christmas box was the photo album which the patients soon put to good use. At 9.30 there was half an hour of carolling over the P.A. system before lights out.

On Christmas Day large boxes of candy were delivered to each ward. The boxes were covered with green tissue paper with a big red tissue paper bow on each side. Inside there were clusters made of Hershey chocolate, raisins and North Pole Candy bars sliced and sprinkled with colourful hard candy. In the afternoon an A.R.C. show was played over the P.A. system for half an hour and at 3.00 Colonel Gantt made his first official broadcast over the P.A. system giving Christmas greetings to all. He introduced Colonel Lehman of the 12th Medical Center who read the Christmas message from President Roosevelt. Anne Carter, the Assistant Field Director, wished Merry Christmas to everyone on behalf of the Red Cross and the broadcast finished with Ave Maria song by one of the medical officers.

Over Christmas many of the patient's thoughts turned to home and the Red Cross had a number of social cases to help the patients with, family problems being prevalent. One unhappy situation the girls had to deal with was wives back in the U.S. asking for divorce and another was resolving the paternity of children born to wives while the soldiers were in Europe. One patient, referred to the Red Cross by the chaplain, was extremely anxious to get married by proxy to his girlfriend back in the States who he had discovered was pregnant. He was anxious that his problem was not discovered back home but after several interviews he consented to write to his fiancée and advise her to go, without the knowledge of her parents, to the Red Cross Chapter in her home town and get help.

Other patients with leg and arm amputations were visited almost daily by the Red Cross who tried to help them adjust to their disability. The girls found that much of the casework involved:

> "...*being a good listener and letting the patient get things off his chest.*"
> (155th General Hospital Red Cross Archives)

Most casework was carried out on a 'brief service basis' because of the short amount of time each patient spent at the hospital. In many instances case work had just begun when the patient was transferred.

At the beginning of 1945 the Recreation Hall underwent two months of redecoration during which time it was closed. At the end of March the redecoration was complete and a party held to celebrate. Unfortunately the patients had only a limited time to enjoy the décor of the hall as by this time the hospital had received orders to close down.

G.I. at the 155th holding up newspaper with news of V.E. Day. (Paul Simmons)

On V.E. Day most of the patients had a pass to go into town but for those who stayed on site the girls put on a movie matinee and everyone was invited to the Red Cross building to hear the Prime Minister's speech. The Mess baked two huge layer cakes decorated with the words 'V.E. Day' and hot chocolate was sent to patients confined to their beds. The day ended with a U.S.O. show.

Those that did venture into Malvern found dancing in the streets, the ringing of church bells and giant searchlights making Victory V signs in the night sky. There was a dance at the winter gardens and sailors from H.M.S. Duke were to be found jumping in and out of the pond in Priory Park. Stewart Trigg remembers that there was an unexpectedly impressive display of fireworks when somebody accidentally got a spark into a box of fireworks.

On June 16 the patients were evacuated and the girls started packing up ready to leave. Some Red Cross equipment was sent for the 93rd to use on Site One. And some to the 52nd and 53rd General Hospitals at Wolverley and Merebrook respectively. After the patients left the girls still found their services in demand with the enlisted men of the unit. Even the officers and nurses used the Red Cross as an information bureau until they left.

Chapter 10

Welcome in their Country

Although the men and women working at the hospitals worked long shifts and had little time for recreation most found time to visit the local towns of Malvern and Worcester. Special booklets were produced by the local councils to provide information on the two towns to American servicemen.

Worcester's booklet welcomed the Americans to the Cathedral city telling them: *"Here you will find much to interest you."* and explaining the links between the English city and its namesakes in Massachusetts and New York. It gave the history of the city from the Romans up to the 20th Century with

FOR U.S. ARMED FORCES IN U.K.

Worcester

Photochrome

" On behalf of the citizens of Worcester I extend to American visitors now among us a very warm welcome. Here you will find much to interest you. Our ancient buildings are reminders of our historical associations and of traditions of which we are proud. Our city generally, as a centre of industry and agriculture and as the gateway to some of the most beautiful areas of Britain, is worthy, I think, of your study. May your stay in Worcester be a pleasurable and memorable one."

W G Godsell

MAYOR

descriptions of historic buildings such as the Cathedral, the Guildhall and Worcester Royal Porcelain Works.

Workers' Educational Association. Details from Mr. F. T. W. Lewis, Wilton Road, Malvern.

There are 10 elementary schools and a residential open-air school. The nearest grammar schools are at Hanley Castle and Worcester, and the nearest secondary school at Worcester.

GUIDE AND OTHER BOOKS ON MALVERN AND DISTRICT

Guide Books to Malvern and its districts can be bought at the book shops or seen in the Public Library in Graham Road.

A General History of Malvern (1817), J. Chambers ; *The Story of Malvern* (1911), G. W. Hastings ; *The Malvern Country* (1901), B. C. A. Windle ; *The Geology of Malvernia* (1942), Arthur Bennett ; *Pictures of Nature in the Silurian Region around the Malvern Hills* (1856), Edwin Lees ; *Great Malvern Priory Church* (1914), A. C. Deane ; *The Antiquities of "Moche Malverne"* (1885), J. Nott ; *Malvern Chase* (a novel), W. S. Symonds ; *The Shadow of the Raggedstone* (a novel), Charles F. Grindrod.

The British Council wishes to thank all those who have helped in compiling this series of Informative Pamphlets for U.S. Armed Forces, especially the staffs of the Regional Offices of the Ministry of Information and Officers of the Special Service Section, Headquarters, European Theater of Operations, United States Army.

Printed by Spottiswoode, Ballantyne & Co. Ltd., London, Colchester and Eton

FOR U.S. ARMED FORCES IN U.K.

The Malverns

To all those many Americans among us in Malvern just now I offer a very warm welcome, both on behalf of the local governing body and of the people of the town and district. You will find us all anxious that you should get to know us and to like us ; further, that you may enjoy the attractions of this famous health resort, which, with all modesty, we feel has few equals in beauty of location and surroundings. I hope you may take away with you the most pleasant memories of the town and that in the days of peace a great many of you may return to experience that larger measure of hospitality and local facilities which we shall then be able to extend to you.

W. J. C. KENDALL, CHAIRMAN MALVERN URBAN DISTRICT COUNCIL

The Malvern booklet stated that the local people hoped that the Americans would:

> *"…enjoy the attractions of this famous health resort, which, with all modesty, we feel has few equals in beauty of location and surroundings."*
> (Guide to Malvern)

The Malvern local council emphasized the beauty of the surrounding area, describing it as a 'Little Switzerland' and the 'Queen of the inland health resorts':

> *"…possessed of nine miles expanse of hills, everywhere accessible and commanding magnificent views over fourteen counties invigorating air and water famous from time immemorial, it attracts visitors from all over the world."* (Guide to Malvern)

The personnel of the 19th General Hospital were clearly impressed by the olde worlde aspect of Malvern. Its archivist describes:

> *"…the thatched cottages, the black and white Tudor houses, the flowers of a brilliance and profusion that the American amateur gardner saw only in his dreams; the peaceful pubs where the labourer played darts and drank his pint of bitter; the general slow tempo of*

English living … there was much to see that was unlike our sprawling energetic land." (19th General Hospital Archives)

Ruth Gregg, nurse at the 93rd General Hospital, describes a day out in the countryside around Malvern to her fiancé back in the States:

" *Towards the middle of the afternoon we got thirsty, and so, not liking to stop at one of the little farm houses, we parked our bikes in front of a little broken down school house and started to use the pump. It took us only two seconds to realise the pumping would do us no good so we started to investigate. There, in the top part of the pump were huddled four baby birds – vintage unknown. I presume they'd been using the spout as a means of entrance and exit. How sweet they looked nestled in there, we forgot all about being thirsty. The traffic hazards out here are much worse than they were back home. Huge cows with large horns wander up and down the roads unattended and if it weren't for the fact that they have very gentle unassuming eyes I'm sure I'd never stir out of my hut. As it is they stare curiously at me and I stare them down every time but those horns! My goodness if they should ever decide they didn't like you, what* **would** *happen?"* (Ruth Gregg papers)

Charles Fletcher, Supply Sergeant with the 90th, recalls that Malvern introduced him to a number of 'firsts'. One of these was drinking hot tea with milk instead of cold tea with lemon and sugar. He remembers:

"It didn't take me long to like it this way and after 63 years I still drink hot tea."

Another first for Charles was fish and chips. He recalls:

"There was something about those fish and chips that made the taste better than the ones I had back home. It may have been the ink from the newspaper print that they were wrapped in."

Something that Charles did find difficult to accept in Malvern was the number of Italian P.O.W.s from a camp at Ledbury who worked on the farms and in the quarries of the surrounding area. He found it difficult to understand why they were not guarded and had the freedom to move around as they pleased. He noticed that they never ventured into the towns or local pubs and surmised that this was because they were afraid of the many American soldiers in the area. He learnt later that a number of the P.O.W.s married local girls and never returned to their own country after the war.

The Plough. (Paul Simmons)

The local pubs in Worcester became a favourite 'hangout' for Charles:

> *"...not only for the may different kinds of beer but the friendship of the local people ... . I think they enjoyed my company as well as I did theirs. There was the trading of stories and jokes. ... they always had a good laugh at the way I threw the darts. They were real good at the game. If I was lucky I would hit the board somewhere. Most of the time it was somewhere on the wall well away from the target. ... Some of the men smoked a pipe when they could get tobacco. I soon learned that it was very scarce and expensive. It was easy to purchase pipe tobacco in our P.X. and didn't cost very much. ... I would usually take a couple of tins along and give it to my friends. They sure made me feel welcome in their country."*

Paul Simmons of the 155th remembers that The Plough was a popular pub and that he and his friends were treated 'like good friends' there. The Swan in Hanley Swan was another pub visited by the Americans and Walter Lochbaum of the 155th remembers that some officers frequented the Unicorn Pub in Malvern, although it was too expensive for the enlisted personnel.

Dances and concerts were organised in the local town for the benefit of the hospital personnel. The Winter Gardens (now the forum) was often used as a venue. H.M.S. Duke's headquarters in Malvern became the venue for band contest in which nine American hospital bands competed. The 81st General Hospital based in Llandaff won the competition for the smaller bands while the winner in the class for the larger bands was the 825th Convalescent Centre near Coventry.

The Unicorn Pub. (M.Collins)

The Winter Gardens. (Author's Collection)

The Americans also took part in sporting contests in the locality. American football was played on Worcester City's Ground in St.George's Lane and baseball contests were held on Victoria Road Sports Ground in Malvern.

In August 1944 two American baseball teams: The Cardinals and The Rebels played at Victoria Road Sports Ground. Both teams were drawn from the army and included several league players. The match, which was played in aid of Malvern Hospital, raised over £40. The Malvern Gazette reporter commented that:

> "Five hundred people ventured out on a Sunday afternoon to witness – for the majority at any rate – their first game of baseball by two teams of American soldiers. I had heard a great deal about this ball game beforehand: how tough and exciting it was. Personally I thought the half hour spent in limbering up in advance was as exciting as any part of the actual game. … During the game the only exciting moments came when the striker dispatched a worth-while ball to send the runners haring from base to base in a satisfying triple. … The game was not fully understood but the crowd appreciated the fine catches made by the deep fielders and one marvellous one in the last innings by the Cardinal's short stop who had previously dropped a 'sitter'. (Malvern Gazette August 1944)

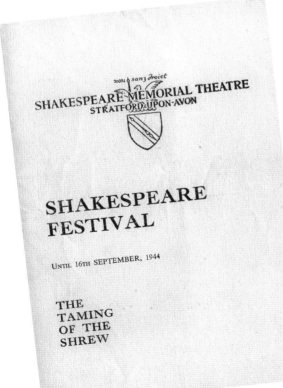

Some of the personnel from the hospitals had the chance to visit Birmingham and Stratford on Avon. Bob Elgin of the 155th remembers that a different Shakespeare play was put on for each night of the week in Stratford. He recalls planning his duties so that he could have a different night off each week and therefore watch all the plays over a seven week period.

When the three day passes were issued personnel could travel as far as London and Edinburgh. Bob Elgin managed a trip to Colwyn Bay in Wales to visit some

Personnel of the 155th on steps of St. Paul's Cathedral in London. L-R- Sgt Bill Lochbaum, Sgt Richard Osgood, Tec4 Sgt Kermit Aumiller, Tec4 Sgt Robert Burns, Sgt Vise Zigrossi.

people he had met previously while awaiting assignment to Blackmore Park. He also spent a three day pass with two friends in Scotland. Paul Simmons remembers that when he went to London on an overnight pass the area was under alert all night because of Buzz Bombs. On another occasion Paul managed to get a pass to go north to Bolton to visit his stepfather's family.

On the whole the people of Malvern made the Americans feel welcome in their town and in an effort to repay them the Americans did what they could for the local children, particularly at Christmas time. Personnel from the various hospitals contributed to parties for the local children. The 5th Hospital Train Unit gave four large boxes of candies and cakes to the orphanage in Great Malvern which the personnel had collected from their rations and boxes received from home. At Christmas 1944 120 children from local schools were treated to a party at the American Red Cross Donut Dugout where the main attractions were an American Santa Claus and presents for all. The hospitals contributed a variety of cakes to the party. John Lisseman remembers the Americans visiting the local schools and putting on shows for the children. He remembers that they were always bought generous amounts of sweets for them.

When the children saw the G.I.s in the locality they would usually ask for sweets with the popular phrase: 'Got any gum chum?' Stewart Trigg remembers that the chewing gum given to the schoolboys would then be used almost as currency. Wendy Grounds (nee Keyte) remembers asking the Americans for chocolate when

Personnel from the 19th General Hospital in London. (Rochester Hospital Archives)

she saw them walking across Poolbrook Common. During the summer months Wendy and her friends picked fruit from their gardens and put them in paper bags to sell for one penny each to the Americans when they walked past her garden into Malvern.

Ruth Gregg remembers meeting a group of youngsters when she went out for a bike ride on the evening of D-Day:

> *"The proverbial question of 'Any gum chum?' came up, so not having any we got the bright idea that we'd come back to camp and take up a collection. We got more stuff than we could carry almost and went back again to their home, 'Home of the Good Shepherd'. [local orphanage] It was just like Christmas watching those children's faces. The headmaster said that they hadn't had an orange in five months. After they'd gorged themselves they showed us all over the dormitories and then came down to the playroom to sing their songs to us. First a hymn and then that 'Mairzy Doats' – what a conglomeration."* (Ruth Gregg Papers)

Ruth and the other nurses were very sad to hear some of the children's stories of how they ended up at the orphanage although they were impressed with the care given to the children there.

During the war Malvern became home to a number of evacuees from Birmingham. Reg Bevan, who came from Selly Oak, remembers standing at the roadside shouting 'Got any gum chum?' when the American army convoys passed by. Reg's hosts, Mr and Mrs Raines, put the camp at Blackmore Park out of bounds to Reg but nevertheless, when he got the chance he and a few of his friends would slip over to the camp to scrounge candy and gum. He remembers:

> *"On one occasion I ate so many cookies I made myself sick. We used to call at one particular Nissen hut where a large coloured man, a cook, I think, used to hand us out hot dogs. After finishing these we would call on our favourite group of soldiers and sit around scoffing and enjoying ourselves."*

He remembers the occasion that he arrived at camp with a broken shoe lace:

> *"One of the soldiers fixed me up with a new one but it was brown and my old ones were black. When I got home Mrs Raines noticed and asked me where I'd got it from; quickly inspiration came to me and I told her I had got it from an old chap who used to call at houses in the area. He rode a bike with a kind of tray in front of the handlebars containing things like needles and pins and various small items."*

Reg Bevan in Malvern with his uncle who was visiting from Birmingham. (R.Bevan)

Unfortunately not all of the children enjoyed good relationships with the American soldiers. In July 1944 three boys aged nine, ten and twelve stole two cycle lamps, some cigarettes valued at 5s.6d and two cycle pumps from a car park in Malvern. The boys were arrested and taken to Malvern Juvenile court. The nine year old admitted taking a lamp and a packet of cigarettes:

> *"Inspector Mound read a police report in which the boy was described as cunning, a liar and not intelligent. He was allowed to run about the streets without restraint until late at night and was the leader of a little gang. Whenever there was mischief in the Malvern Link district the boy was mixed up in it."* (Malvern Gazette)

In his defence the boy told the bench that another boy, who had recently returned to Birmingham, presumably an evacuee, was the ringleader of the group.

> *"Private Thomas Patrick Mullins and Sergeant Anton Edward Colon, whose bikes the children had stolen from, gave evidence against the boys. The nine year old was placed on probation for a year while the ten year old was charged with receiving stolen goods because the twelve year old had given him one of the cycle pumps that he knew was stolen. He was bound over for a year. The magistrate, Mr. A.F. Evans, told his father that the bench felt that he was in with a set of boys who were out*

for mischief and he advised the father to 'break the association'. The magistrate went on to tell the boys that they should not take advantage of American soldiers who were very fond of children and very generous." (Malvern Gazette)

In February 1944 a more serious charge was brought before the court when three young naval stokers violently robbed Sergeant Joe Iverson Lord of the U.S. Army. Sergeant Lord was returning from a dance at the Winter Gardens on January 11 when he was attacked from behind by the three stokers who went through his pockets then ran away.

Apparently the three men aged between 17 and 25 had been drinking heavily that night as they were going away the next day. Earlier in the evening an American soldier had asked them to make less noise to which they retorted 'Whose country is it anyway?' The men were obviously feeling annoyance towards the Americans generally when they came across Sergeant Lord who became the butt of their resentment.

Regarding the charge Mr Justice MacNaghten replied:

"How on earth you had this grudge against the Americans passes my comprehension. If there is one thing that is plain beyond words to everybody it is that we in this country owe everything to the Americans. ... anyone in this country should be only too glad to render to those who have come across the sea to join in our common battle, every assistance." (Malvern Gazette)

The two younger men were sent to a Borstal institution for three years while the 25 year old was sentenced to nine months imprisonment.

Another youngster in trouble with the law was a fifteen year old girl from Bromsberrow who was said to be 'fascinated by the Americans'. During 1944 the girl had left home for several periods to sleep rough on Malvern Common. Her father stated that she was well-behaved when at home but fascinated by the Americans. She admitted that she had been sleeping out in a shed on Malvern Common and a local farmer stated that he had found her and another girl under a rick in one of his fields and that they had been there all night.

Superintendent Adams stated that the girl had been associating with U.S. troops. Staff Sergeant Daniel Sullivan explained that he had first met her three months ago when he had shared a taxi with her. Private First Class Orville Van Thomas said that soon after midnight the girl walked up to the guard house at one of the hospitals and was detained there until the police arrived. She said that she had called there to retrieve her pocket book which was later found.

At the police station the girl gave a fictitious name and said that she came from London. P.C. Phyllis Calder said that she was:

"...very dirty and her hair was unkempt. She was only scantily clad in a cotton dress held together by safety pins. The defendant was hungry." (Malvern Gazette)

The girl told the court that she was unwanted at home so she had:

"...spent three days wandering in Ledbury, returning to the mill to sleep. She made money by selling blackberries. Recently she had stayed in a wood living on chestnuts and apples. Her feet were sore and swollen and she was unable to walk." (Malvern Gazette)

Mr Evans, the chairman, decided to dismiss the charge of 'sleeping out' and felt that the trouble arose because she was unhappy at home. Although the bench felt that the girl was in need of care and protection they decided to send her to a remand home for 28 days and then review the situation.

Phyllis Calder, (now Walford) remembers that several prostitutes were brought into the cells at Malvern Police Station. Phyllis was one of the first two policewomen in Malvern and as a Woman P.C. offences relating to women, children and juveniles were her priority. Prostitutes came to Malvern from several parts of the country to ply their trade at the hospitals. There are records of some of them being charged with being in possession of items that had been issued to the American troops like underclothes, blankets and towels. In most cases they had been given away by servicemen who did not have the right to give them away.

In March 1945 two girls aged 18 and 20 were charged with being in possession of U.S. Army stores including blankets, tins of food, ties, underclothing, a torch, forks, spoons, knives and soap. Twenty year old Mary Ann Hurren told the court that she was doing laundry for two American soldiers and that is why the clothes were there but:

"An American soldier stated that the quantity of goods was far in excess of hospitality rations sometimes allowed. The value was £9.7s.3d based on American valuation. There were proper facilities for soldier's laundry to be done on camp." (Malvern Gazette)

Eighteen year old Kathleen Clasen said that two American soldier friends had brought the blankets and were going to take them back. She stated that the soldiers were eating the girl's rations and that is why the girls told them they would have to bring their own. The two girls were each fined £5.

Phyllis Walford recalls that an American Military Police Unit was attached to the civilian Police Station in Lower Howsell Road. This was a detachment of the 769th M.P. Battalion, the first tactical M.P. unit to be assigned to the Western Base Section. Their H.Q. was at Pheasey Farms Replacement Depot, near Birmingham.

22 detachments had been sent from Pheasey to patrol towns, escort convoys and work alongside the British police in the Western Base Section. The standard reply when the 769th were given an unknown assignment was:

> *"No hill is too high for a bunch of steppers, let's go."* (769th M.P. Battalion Archives)

The detachment were based in Malvern until 2 May 1944 when the whole battalion was recalled from their various assignments in the Western Base Section to reassemble at Bristol to prepare for embarkation to the Continent which was carried out at the end of June.

Janet Green and Stewart Trigg remember seeing American M.P.s holding rifles posted on either side of Barclays Bank door when the pay was collected. Janet and her cousin remember watching avidly, thinking that it was 'better than the pictures' although she remembers that the older people found it quite intimidating.

Stewart Trigg remembers the occasion when an American soldier went berserk in W.H. Smiths and chased the manager around the shop. He recalls:

> *"The Snowdrops, the American Military Police, with their white steel helmets, gaiters and belts had effective, if violent, means of dealing with American soldiers who misbehaved."*

Wendy Grounds remembers being shocked at the amount of force used by the M.P.s when rounding up G.I.s who presumably were A.W.O.L. She remembers that they would hit the men over the head with their batons and then bundle them into the back of their jeep. When G.I.s were arrested and forced to spend time at the police station food would be delivered to them from the American camps.

Chapter 11
Ships that Pass in the Night

There were many happier stories of liaisons between the American servicemen and the local Malvern people. Charles Fletcher recently contacted a lady that he had got to know while he was stationed with the 90th General Hospital.

As Supply Sergeant it was necessary for Charles to travel with the laundry to the Court Steam Laundry in the Small Heath area of Birmingham twice a week. This is where he met Brenda, a seventeen year old, who agreed to travel by train to Worcester that Sunday to meet him. Charles asked one of the cooks in the mess hall to make him a picnic of sandwiches, then he borrowed a bike to cycle to the train station where he met Brenda and the couple picnicked on the river bank.

Supply Sergeant Charles Fletcher. (Charles Fletcher)

'Brenda.' (Charles Fletcher)

Charles didn't want Brenda to take things too seriously so he told her that he was married and had a little girl. Although this was not true the photo he showed Brenda was of the girl back home he would eventually marry. Charles managed to see Brenda several times before he left for France. Once in France it was impossible to write as the unit was always on the move. At the end of the war Charles requested leave to travel to England to see Brenda but this was refused and he returned to his home in America. Once back in America, Charles wrote to Brenda but never received a reply.

In December 2006 Charles placed an article in a Birmingham newspaper to see if he could locate Brenda. Two weeks later he received an email from her grandson and shortly after he spoke to Brenda and members of her family on the phone.

Heather Hill nee Acock, was a British Red Cross Nurse at the newly built Ronkswood Military Hospital in Worcester which had been built with American Lease Lend money. She remembers that notices about local dances were always posted on the notice board at the hospital, transport was always provided. She recalls:

> *"There was an unwritten law for most of us that we were mainly interested in having a good dancing partner and nothing else was expected on either side."*

Heather's dancing partner was nicknamed Dutch as he was an American of Dutch decent. Dutch had a girlfriend back home and Heather had a boyfriend serving in Burma so the couple had an understanding that the relationship would be just a friendship.

Heather remembers that a nursing friend, Nurse Mundy, and herself were both off-duty one afternoon when Dutch and one of his friends invited them for a day out on the river at Worcester. The girls decided to make up a picnic and spent considerable time and effort making lemonade with fresh lemons and sugar. The girls enjoyed their afternoon with the boys rowing them downstream and then picnicking on the river bank. She recalls:

> *"Mundy and I proudly produced our lemonade which was not too bad until the men folk said 'Have some of **our** drink.' We were amazed and delighted at the glorious taste and the lemonade was quietly poured away into the river. What was that wonderful drink we had from the Americans? It was my first sight and taste of coke!"*

The period before D-Day was very busy at Ronkswood Hospital. Hundreds of dressing and cotton swabs were made in preparation for the large influx of patients. On 6 June Heather was off duty and sitting in Cadena Café in Worcester having a coffee when she heard the announcement that the allies had landed in Normandy.

Heather Hill, Red Cross Nurse at Ronkswood Hospital. (Heather Acock)

She left her coffee, jumped on her bike and went straight to the hospital. Of course the wounded did not arrive straight away but before long the wards were full of badly wounded British soldiers from the front, some flown straight from the beaches to Defford Airfield and then driven to Ronkswood by ambulance.

When Heather had time to enquire about Dutch and his friends she was told that they had all gone 'Down South' and she didn't hear from him again. It is possible that he was with the 19th or 90th General Hospitals that went over to France shortly after D-Day to set up hospitals on the Continent. Heather thought of her wartime friendship as 'ships that pass in the night'.

Pam Drew, nee Leach, echoes this statement. She lived opposite the Plough Inn and her parents befriended a number of Americans from the hospital and also from Eastnor Park, where a unit of black soldiers was billeted. One G.I. Larry Lazero, an Italian American who came from Brooklyn, would often bring large pieces of meat for the family which was very much appreciated.

Like Heather, Pam and three friends would often go dancing with a group of Americans at the Drill Hall in Ledbury. One of the friends, Jean, eventually married one of the Americans. Another American, Herbert Rickheimer, or Ricky as he was known, was an orderly at one of the hospitals and Pam remembers that on one occasion he had to cancel a date as he was needed to assist with an operation to amputate a leg.

Pam remembers the occasion when her mother baked a cake for Ricky's birthday on August 4th and asked her to deliver it. On the way eighteen year old Pam sat for a while in the park holding the cake and this is where she met twenty two year old Luther Warren who asked her if she was waiting for someone who hadn't turned up. He offered to carry the cake to the station for her. Luther was a patient at one of the hospitals. He had been hit by a bullet which went through his leg and came out the other side. When they arrived at the station Pam realized that she did not even know his name but she felt that it was love at first sight.

From that moment on Pam saw as much of Luther as possible. She would return home from work and then go straight out to meet Luther, sometimes going to a dance at the Winter Gardens and sometimes going to the Malvern picture house.

Unfortunately, when Luther's wound healed he was sent back into combat although he was reluctant to go. He wrote frequently from the Continent and when he had leave he travelled back to England to visit Pam. Unfortunately Pam's mother did not approve of her daughter's relationship with the American and she refused to put him up for the night although there was room in the house.

The next morning Pam set out to see Luther off the train, although she did not know it, it would be the last time she saw him. When he left Pam was distraught. Luther had told her that he wanted to ask her to marry him but he felt that their backgrounds were too different. Pam felt that he thought he wasn't good enough for her family.

Once back with his unit Luther wrote for a while but then the letters stopped and Pam wonders if he was killed. She wrote to his home in Atlanta but didn't hear anything. Although Pam later married and had a family she still thinks about Luther and wonders what might have been if he had returned to her at the end of the war.

Marriage in Priory Church, Malvern of Sergeant Russom. (Walter Lochbaum)

Some liaisons between G.I.s and English girls did lead to marriage. In 1944 there were twelve marriages at the church of Our Lady and St. Alphonsus between American personnel and English and Irish girls. Sergeant Russom from the 155th General Hospital married an English girl at the Priory Church in Malvern. His best man was Staff Sergeant Willoughby, also of the 155th. After the wedding the couple lived together in an apartment in Malvern.

Private George Butler from Illinois, a cook with the 19th, met eighteen year old Pat Sutton at a dance at the Winter Gardens. Pat was there with a group of friends when George asked her to dance. They were married at Trinity Church in Malvern. George's best man was Private Ken Davis and Pat's two attendants were Evelyn Handy and Eileen Warner. Evelyn wore Royal blue satin and Eileen wore mauve satin. Both carried a bouquet of mauve and pink tulips. Pat had an oyster satin dress and carried a bouquet of arum lilies. The reception was held at The North Malvern Hotel, where there was a 'proper' cake. Unfortunately the couple split up a few months after the 19th went to France.

Several 'All American' marriages were celebrated in Malvern. Lieutenant Louise Beattie, a nurse with the 19th, married Lieutenant John Hancher, an American flying officer, at Christ Church. She was in uniform, as was her bridesmaid Lieutenant Mary Thompson. Her colleagues had brought her pink lilies and pale yellow daffodils which were divided amongst the Westminster Hotel where the honeymoon was taken and the nurses Recreation hall at Blackmore Park Site One, where the reception was held. The reception hall was decorated with flowers and evergreens, the centre piece being a huge floral bell suspended over a three tier wedding cake made in the camp.

Pte. Butler and Miss Sutton

Private G. Butler and Miss P. Sutton

The Rev. R. D. Daunton-Fear officiated at the wedding at Holy Trinity Church, Malvern, of Miss Patricia Sutton, fourth daughter of Mrs. E. S. Sutton, of Valley View, North Malvern, and Private George Butler, of the United States Army.

Given away by her uncle, Mr. H. Buckton, of Birmingham, the bride was dressed in oyster satin and carried a bouquet of arum lilies. Her two attendants were Miss Evelyn Handy and Miss Eileen Warner. The former was in royal blue satin and Miss Warner in mauve satin. Their bouquets were of mauve and pink tulips.

Private Ken Davis, of the U.S. Army, was best man.

The hymns, "Lead us, Heavenly Father" and "Love Divine," were sung. A reception was held at the North Malvern Hotel, attended by a large number of guests.

Malvern Gazette.

Several nurses from the 93rd General hospital were married in Malvern. In May 1945 2nd Lieutenant Shirley N. Craig was married at the post chapel which had recently been redecorated with panel boards and paint. Shirley married 1st Lieutenant Paul Carlson of the engineers, a former patient at the hospital. The bride, who wore a white satin gown, was given away by Colonel Merikangus, the Commanding Officer. The reception took place in the Red Cross Building. 1st

Lieutenant Susan M. Yeager and 2nd Lieutenant Marcella Reckart were also married to American service men in 1945.

Some alliances between English girls and American servicemen did not end in marriage and this was sometimes because the serviceman was already married. Lorraine's Etheridge's Father, Eric Poehl, was in this situation. Lorraine's mother was also married when Lorraine was conceived and a friend of the family remembers how shocked her mother's husband was when he returned home from serving with the Worcesters in Anzio to find that she had been born.

Lorraine herself did not realise that the man who had brought her up was not her father until April 1990 when her elder brother started to research the family tree. Lorraine had only the shortened copy of her birth certificate so she phoned the Malvern Registrar to request the longer form which had more details on it. The Registrar's office bluntly told Lorraine that she must be illegitimate as her father's name was missing from the form. Lorraine found this strange as her mother had been married eight or nine years when she was born. She then realized that her English father had been away fighting at the time of her conception.

When challenged her mother would only tell her that she and Lorraine's father had met at a dance at the Winter Gardens and that she didn't know him well but Lorraine's god mother and mother's sister in law recalled a number of parties at the house when he was present. Later Lorraine found out that her mother knew Eric well enough to contact his wife back in America and that the couple had divorced four times because of the affair with her mother.

Lorraine's mother did inform her that she had been named for the place in France where Eric was serving at the time of her birth. Eric had travelled over to France with the 19th General Hospital in August 1944. Armed only with her father's name and a number, which later turned out to be his house number, she attempted to trace her father. She made little progress until the American Embassy gave her the contact details of 'Trace', an organisation that helped to trace G.I. fathers. With the help of Trace in five months she located her father's family. Sadly her father had died ten years previously but she was able to contact family members who made her feel welcome when she visited her father's home in Burlington, Iowa.

Eric Poehl. (Lorraine Etheridge)

Chapter 12

A Fond Farewell

The end of the war in Europe brought the closure of the hospitals in the Malvern area. The 93rd and 155th prepared to return to the U.S., the 155th with the intention of relocating to the Pacific Theatre of War.

Malvern was sad to see its visitors leaving and the Troops Welfare Committee gave several farewell parties. In June 1945 a farewell dinner was given by Major W.C. Kendall, chairman of Malvern Urban District Council at the County Hotel. After the toasts and the singing of the respective national anthems Major Kendall gave a speech mentioning to the audience that the British Isles had only been invaded twice in the last 888 years, once in 1066 by the Normans and now by the Americans. He added:

> *"Here in Malvern your coming has added a proud chapter to the history of our town and future generations will be shown, perhaps from the hills, the five points where lives have been saved and where maybe some of the greatest marvels of American medical science have been discovered."* (Malvern Gazette 9/6/1945)

Colonel Lehman replied that the Americans had come to love Malvern and England. They had been 'warned' about the English before coming –

> *"...but has not found them reserved or too dignified but very friendly."* (Malvern Gazette 9/6/1945)

After the evening's entertainment Colonel Lehman wrote to Major Kendall and the Council to thank them for their hospitality to him and his officers and nurses. He wrote:

> *"We have always considered ourselves most fortunate to have been stationed in such a beautiful spot to contribute our small part to your noble and commendable support of the war effort. ... Our group will*

ever remember the many kindnesses of your people, your hospitalities and the continued efforts of all groups to make our stay here one of the most pleasant sojourns of our life." (Malvern Gazette 7/7/1945)

Malvern Gazette

Colonel J. C. Miller and Officers of the 12th Medical Centre, U.S. Army, with their hosts, the Malvern Welfare Committee for the Troops—"Au revoir" party at Malvern, July 11th, 1945

Malvern Gazette.

In July there was another party, this time at the Winter Gardens. Captain Roy Limbert, Chairman of the Troops Welfare Committee gave a speech explaining that he viewed the Americans' departure with mixed feelings, sad to see them go but looking forward to having the opportunity to 'cross the big water' to meet up in the States. He emphasised that their friendships:-

"...must surely never die, nor even languish." (Malvern Gazette 14/7/1945)

Many of the Americans also viewed their departure with mixed feelings. Colonel Merikangus, Commanding Officer of the 93rd wrote in his report for 1945:

"The relationships with the British civilians have been cordial and pleasant for most of the personnel of this installation. Improvement of Anglo American relationships have constantly been the theme and several of our duty personnel, as well as patients, have married girls of the United Kingdom." (93rd General Hospital Archives)

U.S. HOSPITAL MOVES OUT

Staff Thanks To Malvern For Hospitality

Another U.S. hospital, the 93rd, left Malvern on Sunday for new quarters at Stafford. The hospital unit, while stationed at Blackmore Park Malvern Wells cared for thousands of patients, and was one of the two such units visited by the Princess Royal when she came to the district earlier in the year. The first Commanding Officer, Col. Merikangus, left some few weeks ago, and he was succeeded by Col. Johnson, who has moved with the unit and who during his short time in the Malverns expressed his pleasure at the friendliness he had experienced. It was Col. Johnson who, hearing that the neighbouring Dutch camp was without a cook, offered to lend one of his staff to fill the post for a while.

Among the personalities who became popular locally while they were with the unit were Miss Duffey, the head of the Red Cross Club Welfare work, who, with Miss Keener, her assistant, attended many local functions and was always ready to help to staff stalls at Red Cross and other money-raising efforts. Capt. Kahl, the head surgeon, and Capt. Cohen, and Chaplain W. H. Rittenhouse who while in Malvern preached at several churches, including the Priory.

THANKS FOR HOSPITALITY

A typical expression of thanks to Malvern for its hospitality came to the "Gazette" Office this week from Sergt. Alan A. Katz, of the hospital's public relations department. Sergt. Katz wrote as follows:

"I am leaving Malvern now, and it is difficult grasping that thought. I feel almost as I did on leaving home. Your town and the people in it have come to mean much to me. And now that I am going I want to bid farewell to all my friends, yet I hardly know what to say. I thank the people of Malvern for the kindness and graciousness that characterised their every activity. Shall I thank them

Sergt. Katz.

for that innate hospitality that caused them to share everything they had with us, or shall I simply say 'Thank you' for having been such true friends?

It is difficult to find words adequately to express what I feel. However, perhaps they will understand if I simply tell them that I do appreciate most deeply everything they have done, and that I shall never forget it."

THE AMERICAN HOSPITALS

Have Become Part of Local Life

A GREAT feature of life in Malvern during the past two or three years has been the establishment of five U.S. hospitals, part of the 12th Medical Centre, under the direction of Col. Lehmann, assisted by Col. Miller, and with the following Commanding Officers at each: Col. Merikangus, Lt.-Col. Smith, Lt.-Col. Gant, Lt.-Col Gill and Lt.-Col. Wayne Brandstadt.

These hospitals are familiar landmarks from the hills, and are built on the plan approved for all emergency hospitals. Wonderfully equipped, they have accommodated thousands of U.S. patients, and from time to time British and even enemy wounded. Of course, censorship regulations forbade any mention of the location of these great establishments in newspapers, and the hospitals always had to be referred to as "in Worcestershire."

The Americans soon established friendly relations, and hospital parties, to which local people were invited, have become a feature. Major Kendall and other members of the Council attended these, and in return Malvern Civic Reception Committee has organised parties at the Winter Gardens for staff and patients. Officers and nurses made friends rapidly and take part in many locally organised social functions. The increasing number of Anglo-American weddings has testified to the permanent character of some of the friendships formed amongst Malvern people—Mrs. Wheeler in particular — have organised a "flower service" through which wards were brightened, and Mrs. Guy Lea and the W.V.S. have initiated a "help service" with 100 volunteers to undertake such duties as reading to patients, mending, looking after the library, doing clerical and other work.

The hospitals have received many distinguished visitors, among them, earlier in the year, the Princess Royal as Chief of the A.T.S. The Princess met Lt.-Col. Resch, head of the U.S. nurses, and said at that time to be the only woman colonel in the country.

Another appreciated visitor was Professor Alexander Fleming, the discoverer of penicillin, which has been used so extensively in the hospitals

MALVERN IS "IDEAL"

The visitor to these hospitals is impressed with their efficiency and with their "world within a world" atmosphere. Some of the finest surgeons in the U.S. are here, and skilled nursing attention is given.

One hospital has been given up to nerve cases, and important sections of others has been the plastic surgery departments in which skin grafting plays a great and healing role.

Nearly all the hospitals have had wonderful views of the hills and patients and staff have said what an ideal place Malvern is, both in air and scenery.

One hospital boasts that in its two years of service only about six lives have been lost.

Malvern Gazette 12/5/1945.

Sergeant Alan Katz, also of the 93rd wrote to the Malvern Gazette to say:

"I am leaving Malvern now and it is difficult grasping that thought. I feel almost as I did on leaving home. Your town and your people in it have come to mean much to me. … I hardly know what to say. I thank the people of Malvern for the kindness and graciousness that characterised their every activity." (Malvern Gazette 11/8/1945)

Malvern Gazette.

Paul Simmons of the 155th, looking back on his time at Malvern says:

"I was 19 years of age, but I never was homesick. It was a great experience and I was proud to be able to serve."

Charles Fletcher who was with the 90th, talks about his time in Malvern as being one of the greatest learning experiences of his overseas assignment. Over 60 years later he states:

"I shall never forget the people and kindness shown towards me."

Once the Americans had left, there was a new dilemma as to whom or what would fill the five vacated hospital sites. One of the ideas was that they could be used as Prisons for German Prisoners of War.

Site at Merebrook used by the Royal Engineers c1950s. (J.C.Geeves)

Dutch soldiers moved into the site at Wood Farm as soon as it was vacated by the Americans and later it was used for Displaced Persons from Latvia, Lithuania, Estonia and the Ukraine. Eventually it reverted back to its original use as part of Worcestershire Golf Course. The Royal Engineers took over the site at Merebrook in1946 and remained there until 1958. The SAS (Special Air Service) was based there for a few months in 1959. When the British forces left the site most of the wartime buildings were demolished by Worcestershire County Council, a handful being left for industrial use. The Officers' Mess was used as a riding school for a while. Brickbarns was taken over by the Ministry of Health for use as a tuberculosis hospital although it was necessary to make a number of alterations to the site first. Later it became St. Wulstan's Psychiatric Hospital and now there is a housing estate and nature reserve on the site.

St Wulstans Hospital on site of Brickbarns. (Judges Postcards)

This left the two hospitals at Blackmore Park vacant. There were rumours that the Admiralty and Ministry of Aircraft Production were interested in the sites. Site One was used temporarily as a German Prisoner of War Camp, designated Camp Number 689, and the Navy used Site Two for a short time.

By May 1946 one of the Blackmore sites was still vacant as this poem published in the Malvern Gazette illustrates:

> *"Five U.S. hospitals that all Malvern saw,*
> *The Dutch came and conquered and then there were four.*
> *Four U.S. hospitals the army came to see,*
> *The R.E.s moved in and then there were three.*
> *Three U.S. hospitals still rather new,*
> *The county beat the Council and then there were two.*
> *Two U.S. hospitals standing in the sun,*
> *The Navy liked Blackmore and then there was one.*
> *One U.S. hospital where no one seems to go,*
> *Nine months empty – does Mr. Bevan know?"*
> (Malvern Gazette 25/5/1946)

In December 1947 both sites at Blackmore Park became a training Centre for the Pioneer Corps. The strength of the Training Camp fluctuated between 500 and 1500 and in 1949 the personnel moved to Saighton Camp in Chester. Around this time a R.E.M.E. Training Battalion started using the camp and in 1955 there is reference to Site Two being used by an amalgamation of the 9 and 11 Training Battalion while Site One was to be reopened to provide a training area for vehicle mechanics. During this time the ward buildings were adapted for use as garages by insertion of large doorways in the ends and sides of the ward blocks. In 1956 the unit closed down and the training was moved to various other training battalions.

During the 1970s the site was squatted by travelling families whilst in ownership of the County Council. Rapid deterioration of the buildings due to vandalism resulted in the creation of a new purpose built gypsy camp which is situated alongside the driveway to Site One.

Nowadays the evidence of the site's role in World War Two is fast disappearing. Site One has been used as an industrial estate but is now awaiting redevelopment despite opposition from local residents. Site Two is being used as a caravan park, part of which is for the Girl Guiding Movement. Most of the wartime buildings were demolished in the 1970s.

Walter (Bill) Lochbaum salutes at the entryway to what remains of Site Two 1985. (Walter Lochbaum)

Some evidence of the American presence remains in the area. The door to the cloisters of Our Lady and St. Alphonsus Church near Blackmore Park was bought with money from the Americans stationed at Blackmore Park. It is said locally that the Americans were not allowed through the main door of the church wearing side arms so they paid for a door to be made from the churchyard to the cloisters. Just inside a rack was made for the soldiers to place their guns while in the church.

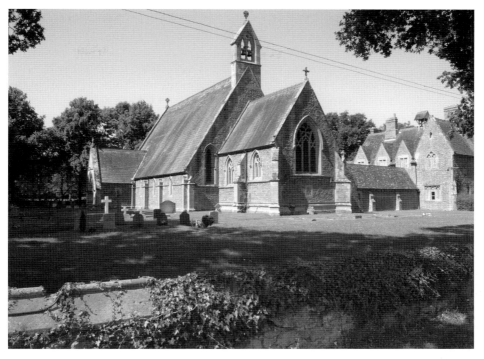

Catholic church of Our Lady of Peace and St. Alphonsus showing cloister door paid for by Americans at Blackmore Park. (M.Collins)

In January 1950 a fund was launched to provide a plaque commemorating the role of the American hospitals in the Malvern district. There was a public meeting and a vote was taken on its position. It was voted 10 – 7 that the plaque should be placed in the Winter Gardens. For the Malvern Gazette the move was 'long overdue' as it wanted to see more done to commemorate the part played in the war of the various military units in Malvern:

> *"We still think the Council, as the town's officially elected body should devise some project whereby in one central place visitors and residents in many years to come may see a chronological record of the way that Malvern once became a haven and a training ground for the forces of freedom … a plaque, while welcome, would never sum up the happy memories of the American 'occupation'.*
>
> *How can a bronze tablet and some words, however well chosen, record the essential charm with which the Americans became one with so many local families; how they shared their rations with many; how they helped in money raising efforts for good causes; unofficially adopted the boys of a local home; … of the ready way their chaplains took duty in local churches of all denominations; how romances flourished or how one C.O. said goodbye to the district by flying over it with a British Air Vice-Marshall. These and a hundred kindred acts endeared them to us all."* (Malvern Gazette)

The plaque can now be seen in the Malvern Museum.

Plaque to be found in Malvern Museum. It reads: This memorial erected by the people of Malvern commemorates seven American General Hospitals with ten thousand beds and the 12th General Hospital Center. Situated near Malvern 1943-45 during the World War.

View of the surgical Wards 93rd General Hospital 2007. (M.Collins)

Gable end Ward Building 93rd General Hospital 2005. (M.Napthan)

Ward building 93rd General Hospital 2005. (M.Napthan)

Interior of Wards showing concrete frames 93rd General Hospital 2005. (M.Napthan)

Interior of Wards showing metal frames 93rd General Hospital 2005. (M.Napthan)

93rd General Hospital Former X-ray building 2005. (M.Napthan)

Last remaining Nissen hut 93rd General Hospital 2005. (M.Napthan)
(Demolished 2007)

View from Operating Theatre Corridor 93rd General Hospital 2006. (M.Collins)

Casualty Reception building 93rd General Hospital 2005. (M.Napthan)

Remains of the vehicle ramp 93rd General Hospital 2007. (M.Collins)

Covered walkway 93rd General Hospital 2005. (M.Napthan)

93rd General Hospital 2005. (M.Napthan)

Post war REME sign entrance to admin site 93rd General Hospital. (M.Napthan)

Demolition 93rd General Hospital Buildings 2007. (M.Collins)

155th General Hospital building serving as reception office for the caravan site. (Now demolished) (M.Collins)

155th General Hospital c.1970s. (Worcestershire County Council via M.Napthan)

155th General Hospital c.1970s. (Worcestershire County Council via M.Napthan)

Ward buildings 155th General Hospital c. 1970s. (Worcestershire County Council via M.Napthan)

155th General Hospital Covered Walkway c.1970s. (Worcestershire county Council via M.Napthan)

Abbreviations

A.R.C. – American Red Cross
AWOL – Absent Without Leave
C.O. – Commanding Officer
H.Q. – Headquarters
E.T.O. – European Theatre of Operations
P.T.O. – Pacific Theatre of Operations
G.W.R. – Great Western Railway
L.M.S. – London, Midland and Scottish Railway
M.P. – Military Police
N.C.O. – Non-commissioned officer
Col. – Colonel
Cpl. – Corporal
Lt. – Lieutenant
Maj. – Major
Pfc – Private First Class
Pvt. – Private
Sgt. – Sergeant
Tec.4 – Technician 4th Grade
P.O.W. – Prisoner of War
Px. – Post Exchange – U.S. equivalent of NAAFI
R.A.F. – Royal Air Force
W.V.S. – Women's Voluntary Service – British civilian voluntary organisation
Comm. Z. – Communication Zone – area behind the combat zone i.e. U.K.
Z.I. – Zone of the Interior (U.S.)

Glossary

Ambulatory – patients able to walk.

Assigned – having permanent duties at a base.

Limited Assignment – having temporary duties at a base.

Convalescent Hospitals – (C.H.) – Treated convalescing troops sent from station or general hospitals.

General Hospital – (G.H.) – Hospitals with 1082 beds (although at times when the need arose this number was larger). Mainly intended for soldiers wounded during combat.

Station Hospitals – (S.H.) – Hospitals with 834 beds serving the needs of troops in training. Often attached to a base.

Operation Overlord – Codename for Allied invasion of France.

Operation Bolero – Codename for the build up of troops in Britain in readiness for D.Day.

Mess hall – dining room.

Motor Pool – Unit that repaired and maintained the vehicles attached to a unit.

Special Service – Education and Entertainment section responsible for the morale of troops on a base.

Western Base Section – Western quarter of U.K.

Appendix 1

American Military Units known to be in Malvern 1943-45

Blackmore Park
701st Medical Sanitation Co. - March 1944
19th General Hospital Medical Detachment - Sep. '43 - May '44
19th General Hospital Detachment of Patients - Sep. '43 - May '44
769th Military Police Battalion (ZI) Company A, Detachment A
137th Army Postal Unit
93rd General Hospital - May '44 - Sep. '45
Detachment of Patients 4172 Hospital Plant
Detachment of Patients 4173 Hospital Plant
90th General Hospital - March '44 - July '44
65th General Hospital - Oct. '43 - March '44
155th General Hospital - July '44 - July '45
255th Medical Detachment
256th Medical Detachment
374th M.P. patrol Unit
114th Army Postal Unit Type A
115th Army Postal Unit Type A
3960th Signal Switchboard Detachment

Merebrook
53rd General Hospital HQ - Mar. '44 - Sep. '45
53rd General Hospital Medical Detachment
Detachment of Patients 4175 Hospital Plant

Wood Farm
55th General Hospital - Jan. '44 - May '45
Detachment of Patients 4176 Hospital Plant

Brickbarns
56th General Hospital - Oct. '43 - Feb. '44
96th General Hospital - Feb. '44 - July '45
312th Station Hospital - July '45 - Aug. '45
231st Station Hospital - Sep. '45
Detachment of Patients Hospital Plant 4174

Malvern Link
5th Hospital Train Unit
12th Medical Hospital Center
66th Army Postal Unit
106th Finance Distribution Unit
121st Army Postal Unit

Appendix 2a

Army Hospital Centers

Hospital Center	Hospital Group	Place	Date of Activation
12	5	Malvern	April 1944
15	4	Cirencester	April 1944
801	1	Taunton	Feb. 1945
802	2	Blandford	Feb. 1945
803	3	Devizes	Feb. 1945
804 (Originally 6801 provisional-activated June 1944)	6	Whitchurch	Feb. 1945
805	7	Newmarket	Feb. 1945

N.B. Hospital Groups designated October 1944

Appendix 2b

U.S Army Hospitals in U.K   August 1944

Plant No.	Site	Hospital Unit	Plant No.	Site	Hospital Unit
4100	Truro	314SH	4154	Blockley	327SH
4101	Tavistock	115SH	4155	Moreton	
4102	Moretonhampstead ?		4156	Fairford	
4103	Newton Abbot	124GH	4157	Salisbury	152SH
4104	Exeter	36SH	4165	Tyntesfield	74GH
4105	Barnstaple	313SH	4166	Bristol	117GH
4106	Bishops Lydeard	185GH	4167	Stoneleigh	307SH
4107	Norton Manor	101GH	4168	Bromsgrove	123SH
4108	Taunton	67GH	4169	Wolverley	52GH
4109	Axminster	315SH	4170	Bewdley	297GH
4110	Yeovil, Houndstone	169GH	4171	Bewdley	114GH
4111	Yeovil, Lufton	121GH	4172	Blackmore Park	93GH
4112	Sherborne	228SH	4173	Blackmore Park	155GH
4113	Frome St Quintin	305SH	4174	Malvern Wells	96GH
4114	Blandford	22GH	4175	Malvern Wells	53GH
4115	Blandford	119GH	4176	Malvern Wells	55GH
4116	Blandford	125GH	4177	Leominster	135GH
4117	Blandford	131GH	4178	Foxley	123GH
4118	Blandford	140GH	4179	Foxley	156GH
4119	Wimborne	106GH	4180	Kington	122GH
4120	Ringwood	104GH	4181	Kington	107GH
4121	Netley	110SH	4182	Abergavenny	279SH
4122	Winchester	38SH	4183	Rhyd Lafar	81GH
4123	Stockbridge	34GH	4184	Carmarthen	232SH
4124	Odstock	158GH	4185	Lichfield	33SH
4125	Grimsdith	250SH	4186	Shugborough	312SH
4126	Warminster	216GH	4187	Sudbury Derby	182GH
4127	Tidworth	3SH	4188	Whittington	68GH
4128	Perham Downs	103GH	4189	Oteley Deer Park	137GH
4129	Everleigh	187GH	4190	Overton	83GH
4130	Devizes	141GH	4191	Penley	129GH
4131	Devizes	128GH	4192	Iscoyd Park	82GH
4132	Erlestoke Park	102GH	4193	Saighton	109GH
4133	Bath	160SH	4194	Clatterbridge	157GH
4134	Falfield	94GH	4195	Stockton Heath	168SH
4135	Malmesbury	120SH	4196	Davey Hulme	10SH
4136	Lydiard Park	302SH	4197	Glasgow	316SH
4137	Swindon	154GH	4198	Harrogate	115GH
4138	Chiseldon	130SH	4199	Harrogate	116GH
4139	Marlborough	347SH	4200	Mansfield	184GH
4140	Hermitage	98GH	4201	Nocton Hall	7GH
4141	Checkendon	306GH	4202	Allington	348SH
4142	Kingwood	304GH	4203	Thorpe North	303SH
4143	Wheatley	97GH	4204	Diddington	49SH
4144	Headington	91GH	4205	Cambridge	163GH
4145	Middleton Stoney	318SH	4206	Newport	280SH
4146	Ramsden	317SH	4207	Braintree	121SH
4147	Burford	61GH	4208	Acton, Suffolk	136SH
4148	Fairford	186GH	4209	Redgrave Park	65GH
4149	Cirencester	188GH	4210	Wymondham	231SH
4150	Cirencester	192GH	4211	North Mimms	1GH
4151	Daglinworth	111GH	4212		
4152	Stowell Park	160GH	4213	Packington	77SH
4153	Ullenwood	110GH	4261	London	16SH

Acknowledgements

U.K. contributors
Brian Baxter, Reg Bevan, Pat Carter, Tony Clay, Pam Drew, Lorraine Etheridge, Jan Green, Wendy Grounds, Heather Hill, Gill Holt, Anthony Hornyold, Edward Jones, John Lisseman, Diana Medley, Mike Napthan, Ivy Pitt, Jane Ratcliffe, Anne Rasile, Graham Tipping, Stewart Trigg, Neil and Adrian Turley, Phyllis Walford, Mike Webster, Rosemary Williams.

U.S. contributors
John Bowen, Bob Elgin, Charles Fletcher, Daniel Lennox, Walter Lochbaum, Norm Johnson, Michael Samburg, Claire Saxon, Paul Simmons, Jim Bain.

Groups and Publications
Malvern Gazette, Malvern Library, VFW Magazine, Bulge Bugle, Order of the Purple Heart, SHEAF Communiqué, U.S. National Library of Medicine, Chris Nardy and Battleship Cove Museum, Army Medical Journal, Journal of Thoracic Surgery, Phil Maples and Rochester Hospital Archives, Malvern Museum, University Archives and Manuscripts Women's Veteran's Historical Collection, Jackson Library, University of N. Carolina at Greenboro (Mary Grigg Collection), NARA service: 12th Hospital Center Archives, 5th Hospital Train Unit Archives, 19th General Hospital and Red Cross Archives, 53rd General Hospital Archives, 65th General Hospital Archives, 90th General Hospital and Red Cross Archives, 93rd General Hospital and Red Cross Archives, 155th General Hospital and Red Cross Archives.